Praise for *The Colleg*

"A family new to the process will be glad and instructions for essay writing, test ta. aid. Recognizing the value of a range of o ...ors discuss the wisdom of starting at a community college, entering the military first, or, if freshman year isn't working out, transferring from one college to another. Such discussions are rare in books of this kind and thus particularly welcome."   —*The Wall Street Journal*

"Thorough [and] instructive . . . Furda and Steinberg provide a high level of detail, making this volume useful to parents who haven't been through the process before as well as to those familiar with it. A helpful guide for parents with children approaching college age."
                                             —*Library Journal*

"This exceptional guide to your family's college conversation will help you help your teen develop their own ideas about what they want in college."   —*Grown and Flown*

"Eric Furda and Jacques Steinberg are giants in the field of college admissions, so it isn't surprising that they have created one of the best books I have read on navigating the college admissions process. Every parent of middle or high schoolers should read *The College Conversation*, which illuminates and demystifies the process and provides important practical advice for forging partnerships between parents and their children."
    —Marcia Hunt, director of college and academic advising, Pine Crest
       School (Fort Lauderdale, Florida), and former president, National
                Association for College Admission Counseling

"*The College Conversation* brings students and families together with meaningful exercises that help students reflect on their interests and potential. Steinberg and Furda understand the emotional toll of the admissions process and dial down the anxiety. They show how to research schools, navigate financial aid, and even take you behind the scenes in admissions offices after students hit the submit button. This is essential reading for college-bound students and their families."
    —Julie Shimabukuro, ninth and tenth grade principal, John Burroughs
          School, and former director of undergraduate admissions at
                    Washington University (St. Louis, Missouri)

"In *The College Conversation*, Eric Furda and Jacques Steinberg have shared a lifetime of deep experience and wisdom in the college admissions and higher education fields. The authors strike an impressive balance: they offer a rich array of straightforward, practical, realistic, and actionable insights and strategies. Simultaneously, they keep the authentic health, well-being, and thriving of students and families at the core of each chapter. With these shared values, this is the one book that parents, educators, and student advocates need to help their students gain the most from the college admissions journey."

—Ana Rowena McCullough, founder and CEO of QuestBridge

"Finally—a book on college fit that addresses the question of cost as a function of college fit! Eric Furda and Jacques Steinberg provide a thoughtful dissection of the incredibly complex college admissions process in a way that can resonate with school counselors, parents, and students. With a focus on introspection and reflection—from the initial college search to the reality of college cost and its role in the application process, and in the aftermath of understanding admissions decisions—everyone will emerge from this book with a better understanding of how to advise and support students, from our most vulnerable to our most resourced."

—Sara Urquidez, executive director of Academic Success Program (Dallas, Texas)

"Never before has it been so crystal clear that—for the future financial security of students and families—the choice of college must be approached as a value proposition (as much, if not more, than anything else). Steinberg and Furda provide a reassuring road map to coming to a decision that makes your child happy without breaking the bank."

—Jean Chatzky, *New York Times* bestselling author, and CEO of HerMoney

"Finding the right college can be nerve-racking for students and parents alike. But it can also serve as a growing experience for both generations and a lesson in adult decision-making for students. The authors draw on their unique experiences to help families navigate that bizarre and uniquely American rite of passage known as college admissions."

—Edward B. Fiske, editor of *Fiske Guide to Colleges*

PENGUIN BOOKS

THE COLLEGE CONVERSATION

Eric J. Furda is the former dean of admissions at the University of Pennsylvania and the former executive director of admissions at Columbia University. He is the cohost of *The Process*, a SiriusXM program devoted to college admissions and financial aid.

Jacques Steinberg is the *New York Times* bestselling author of *The Gatekeepers* and *You Are an Ironman*, and is a former *New York Times* education journalist. He has served as a senior executive at Say Yes to Education and on the board of the National Association for College Admission Counseling. He appears periodically as a college admissions expert on NBC's *Today* show.

The College Conversation

A Practical Companion for Parents
to Guide Their Children Along the
Path to Higher Education

Eric J. Furda

Jacques Steinberg

PENGUIN BOOKS

PENGUIN BOOKS

An imprint of Penguin Random House LLC

penguinrandomhouse.com

First published in the United States of America by Viking,
an imprint of Penguin Random House LLC, 2020
Published in Penguin Books 2021

ISBN 9781984878366 (paperback)

THE LIBRARY OF CONGRESS HAS CATALOGED THE HARDCOVER EDITION AS FOLLOWS:
Names: Furda, Eric, author. | Steinberg, Jacques, author.
Title: The college conversation: a practical companion for parents to
guide their children along the path to higher education / Eric J. Furda,
Jacques Steinberg.
Description: New York: Viking, [2020] | Includes bibliographical
references and index.
Identifiers: LCCN 2020015460 (print) | LCCN 2020015461 (ebook) |
ISBN 9781984878342 (hardcover) | ISBN 9781984878359 (ebook)
Subjects: LCSH: College applications.
Classification: LCC LB2351.5 .F87 2020 (print) | LCC LB2351.5 (ebook) |
DDC 378.1/616—dc23
LC record available at https://lccn.loc.gov/2020015460
LC ebook record available at https://lccn.loc.gov/2020015461

Printed in the United States of America
1st Printing

Designed by Alexis Farabaugh

In memory of my mother, Virginia, a voracious learner who could not afford the opportunity to attend college, and for my father, Robert, who sacrificed so I had the chance to do so.

—Eric

In memory of my father, Barry, who always set the bar high, and with gratitude to him and to my mother, Edythe, for their support in making my own higher-education dreams come true.

—Jacques

Contents

Introduction

I magine what it's like to be a teenager applying to college at the
outset of the third decade of the twenty-first century.

Arrayed before them is a dizzying menu of more than two
thousand four-year colleges and universities in the United States
alone, several dozen of which admit only a small fraction of those
who apply. A handful of the most exclusive and best known go a step
further and turn away nearly all would-be students. Meanwhile, the
majority of the nation's bachelor's-degree-granting schools, many of
them fine institutions of higher learning flying well below the radar,
offer admission to most applicants. Some of those colleges even strug-
gle to fill their first-year classes each fall, to say nothing of generating
sufficient revenue to keep the lights on or perhaps face the prospect
of shutting their doors.

How can high school juniors or seniors possibly survey—let alone
take the measure of—the offerings across this vast, confusing landscape and figure out where they might fit in?

As they seek to differentiate one campus from the next (and the next), the colleges bombard them with marketing materials, delivered via U.S. mail, email, text message, social media, and sometimes live phone calls from students or even prerecorded robocalls. The schools use contact lists purchased from the College Board, the purveyor of the SAT, as well as from the American College Testing Program (sponsor of the ACT test), which are then customized by students' zip codes, test scores, academic and extracurricular interests, and grades (all reported by the students when they signed up for the test). Day after day throughout their junior year and senior fall, the utility bills in their family's mailbox are crowded out by lush full-color brochures illustrated with panoramic campus photos and punctuated with stats that trumpet measures of student success ("95 percent of our graduates have a job or are enrolled in graduate school within six months of graduation") or satisfaction ("Ranked fifth by *U.S. News & World Report* in the category of 'A-Plus Schools for B Students'"). By early 2020, there were signs of a backlash against these practices, including the filing of a lawsuit by the parent of a Chicago public school student, challenging the sharing of minors' personal data, for profit, with the colleges. But there was no immediate indication of the potential impact, if any, on colleges' recruitment efforts.

Meanwhile, prospective enrollees' email inboxes clog each day at dawn with pop quizzes from their suitors. (Spoiler alert: the correct answer to each question is always the name of the college reaching out to them.) There are also Letterman-inspired top five lists of tips for applying to college; come-ons, including testimonials from famous alumni and odes to creature comforts like Tempur-Pedic mattresses in every dorm room; and so-called fast apps.

The latter are the college admissions world's version of a pre-approved credit card form: a one-page application that has been prepopulated with their name, address, and other personal information that they supplied to the College Board and that was also made available to the colleges for purchase. Opening an envelope emblazoned with designations like "First Priority Scholar," candidates are told that they appear to be such a strong prospect for admission that the standard application fee is being waived, and that in lieu of composing an original essay they need only submit a graded paper from high school. Indeed, all they really need to do is sign on the dotted line. More than a few students who felt buoyed by their first priority designation have been surprised to find themselves later summarily denied by these very institutions—some of them well-known brand names.

Meanwhile, throughout the fall of senior year, representatives from the admissions offices that will consider all these college applications typically spend several months in search of students who might be persuaded to apply to their institutions. Among the objectives of these recruiting trips—whether virtual or in-person—is to identify candidates who would add to the campus community not only by virtue of their academic achievements, life experience, or, in some instances, their ability to pay full freight, but who might also make the admissions process that much more competitive.

Then the tables turn, and it is time for the students applying to make the case for acceptance.

In contrast to the applications their parents may have filled out decades earlier—one at a time, by typewriter or sometimes by hand—they will likely find themselves working through the Common Application, usually referred to as the Common App, which is accepted at more than nine hundred institutions. This platform enables them to save time and effort by typing their personal information on the Common App website just once and to respond to a series of generic essay prompts intended to yield personal statements of several hundred words. These will then be shared with each of the institutions to which they apply that accept the Common Application.

Many of the schools that accept the Common Application also require completion of a series of additional essays, known as a supplement, that are specific to their institution and often intended to gauge the extent of the homework applicants have done about that school and the intensity of their ardor for attending it.

While the Common Application may be the most widely used method of applying to colleges and universities in the United States, it is hardly the only one. By the spring of 2019, 135 institutions had committed to accept the Coalition for College, which they designed collectively with the particular intention of helping low-income and other students historically underrepresented on the nation's college and university campuses. Other application forms that are shared by multiple institutions include the Universal College Application and the Cappex Application.

Regardless of the application they use, the most selective private colleges and universities also put students through an intensive and exhausting evaluation known as the holistic admissions process. When admissions officers use the word "holistic," they mean that they are taking a look at the whole person, as opposed to relying on a mere cutoff on a standardized test or grade point average. It is a process that prizes a rigorous curriculum (ideally including as many Advanced Placement courses as a high school student can handle); a sustained passion for (and demonstrated leadership within) at least a few extracurricular activities; community service; enthusiastic appraisals from teachers and college counselors, as conveyed via their recommendations; socioeconomic, racial, and geographic diversity; and, in many (though no longer all) instances, high scores on the

SAT or its chief competitor, the ACT, to the extent such tests are considered.

For those who wish to score higher on these tests—with a goal of submitting the results, even to those colleges that regard the SAT and ACT as optional—there are any number of in-person and online resources that offer the prospect of a boost, ranging in price from free (including from the College Board itself, in partnership with online Khan Academy) to many thousands of dollars. Because many students don't necessarily perform well on standardized tests, and the value of those tests has been questioned by some educators, including those concerned with making the admissions process more equitable and inclusive, a growing roster of more than one thousand colleges and universities do not require the SAT or ACT—at least for some applicants. The list of test-optional colleges and universities further ballooned during the COVID-19 pandemic, as many students faced challenges to even take a test.

And then there's the matter of figuring out how to pay for it all. Students applying for financial aid and their parents will fill out the FAFSA, the Free Application for Federal Student Aid, which can be as time-consuming and bewildering as an IRS form and which generates the so-called expected family contribution, or EFC, that many colleges and universities will expect a family to pay. (Beginning in the 2022–23 application cycle, the government was expected to phase out the term "expected family contribution" and replace it with "student aid index," a new calculation intended, in part, to boost financial aid to low-income students in particular.) Depending on their annual family income and assets, and whether the school to which they have been admitted offers merit aid in addition to need-based aid—or whether it is an in-state public college or university, or private institution—students and their families could be responsible for paying as little as nothing or as much as nearly $80,000 annually, a figure that includes tuition, room and board, books, travel, and a menu of fees.

No wonder so many first-year college and university students stagger to the starting line at their respective new campuses exhausted, demoralized, confused, and even a bit spooked by a moment that should mark the beginning of something wondrous and invigorating, but can often feel anticlimactic after the many battles just endured.

N ow imagine what it is like to be the parent of a young person applying to college as the third decade of the twenty-first century looms.

Or maybe you don't have to imagine the situation, because you are about to embark on the admissions process or are already in the midst of it.

What do you need to know to help your child navigate this intimidating, often maddening odyssey? How can you best support and guide your child while being careful to ensure (in close consultation with your child) that your lane is clearly marked and that you stay safely within it? What prompts, activities, and other strategies might you draw upon to engage your child in an extended conversation about nothing less than the next chapter of their young lives, conducted at a perilous moment when their brains are changing and their hormones are raging and they are beginning to explore not only who they are but who they wish to become? And how do you do so as many of the disruptions of the pandemic—which upended daily life for students, families, and colleges alike—continue to reverberate?

For young people and their families, the quest for admission has often become an end in and of itself, with surprisingly little thought devoted to what children want to study once they arrive on campus (to say nothing of why) or to whether the institution that is at the top of their wish list offers the optimal conditions for success, as measured by class sizes, support services (such as the availability of tutoring, mentoring and counseling, and financial aid) and whether courses in a desired area of study are even offered.

With so much time and effort devoted to getting in and to making the case (and the grades) for doing so, seventeen- or eighteen-year-olds typically have little time to pause to get to know themselves, or to reflect on their immediate priorities and values, let alone how a postsecondary institution could aid them in achieving their goals for young adulthood. Dazzled by an institution's renowned marquee, or its ranking in publications like *U.S. News*, they (and their parents) may have little inclination to seriously question such choices—or to consider other, less-well-known schools that may be more affordable while still offering a high-quality education.

It is in this spirit that we have written *The College Conversation*, which we intend to be a useful and reliable companion to parents as they guide their children along the pathway to college. While we will often address our advice specifically to parents, there are any number of other adults who play a significant role in a child's life. We hope, for example, that college counselors and other mentors—such as those at community-based organizations—will find information of value in these pages.

Some readers may question whether the world needs another college admissions reference book, considering the small mountain of such titles available. What we've sought to create here is more like a guided meditation, written for parents, and for parents and children to engage in together. Rather than adding to the existing canon of "how to get in" college guides or rankings, our approach is more in the vein of *Difficult Conversations: How to Discuss What Matters Most*, the perennial bestseller by members of the Harvard Negotiation Project, which aspires to provide "a step-by-step approach to having those tough conversations with less stress and more success." *Difficult Conversations* imparts advice on how to "start the conversation without defensiveness" and "listen for the meaning of what is not said," and we suggest ways to blaze similar trails for students and parents embarking on the college process. We also admire the tone of another go-to resource from a far earlier stage in a family's life— *What to Expect When You're Expecting.*

Among our primary objectives is to illuminate, demystify, and inform the often daunting process of applying to college. We do so as a bachelor's degree grows ever more important as the gateway to middle-class life and adult success—especially for those young people who may be mired in generational poverty, and for whom higher education can serve as catalyst for social mobility.

Regardless of the level of your own education, you may be feeling anxious about how your child will fare in this process, as well as whether you are "sufficiently equipped," as parenting expert Carol Sutton Lewis told us, "to be the person to guide them through." We hope this book will give you confidence on both these fronts, along with the understanding that you as a parent aren't going to get everything right and that's OK.

We also want to put the college application into a far broader context—to help parents encourage their children to look beyond the mere mechanics of sorting colleges, taking tests, assembling details about themselves, and making their case for admission. In short, we wish to arm parents with ways to encourage their children to find meaning in their quest and to look deep within themselves to take the measure of who they are, who they would like to become, and how a higher education might facilitate that growth.

Amid the noise and even madness that have come to characterize this process for so many families, we make the case for the restoration of some sanity and calm. As we were reporting and writing this book, in spring 2019, federal prosecutors charged more than four dozen defendants in what they described as "the largest college admissions scam ever prosecuted by the Department of Justice" and later sent some to jail.

We also wish to provide a neon-green road sign reminder of the ultimate goal of a college degree or other postsecondary credential: to prepare a young person for an adulthood that they might variously consider to be successful, engaging, fulfilling, balanced, empathetic, generous, and, in the end, they hope, happy. That said, we readily acknowledge that our mission here is far easier said than done.

Together, we bring to this task more than a half century of combined professional experience and expertise.

Eric served from 2008 to 2020 as the dean of admissions of the University of Pennsylvania, and from 1996 to 2004 as executive director of admissions of Columbia University, two Ivy League institutions that are among the nation's most selective colleges and universities. During his last full cycle as dean, the University of Pennsylvania received more than 42,000 applications for about 2,400 seats in the undergraduate Class of 2024. Eric is also a former chairman of the board of the Common Application. Since 2016 he has hosted *The Process*, a popular college admissions show on SiriusXM satellite radio, and has had a long-running blog (*Page 217*). He is a former scholarship committee member for the Lenfest Scholars Foundation, a nonprofit organization that provides financial support to public high school students going on to college from rural areas of south-central and southeastern Pennsylvania. In early 2021, he joined the college counseling team at the William Penn Charter School, an independent school in Philadelphia.

For most of the quarter century he worked at *The New York Times*, Jacques covered education, including roles as the paper's national education correspondent and senior editor for education initiatives. He is the author of *The Gatekeepers: Inside the Admissions Process of a Premier College* (2002, with a revised edition in 2012), a *New York Times* bestseller and a *New York Times* Notable Book now in its twenty-eighth printing. It is a narrative account of the college admissions process that follows an admissions officer at Wesleyan University, as well as a half dozen applicants, for an entire year.

From 2013 until the summer of 2020, Jacques led a compact of 120 private colleges and universities as a senior executive at Say Yes to Education, a pioneering nonprofit organization that partners with cities that have a critical mass of families from low-income and other backgrounds historically underrepresented on college campuses. The organization's goal is to see that every public school student not only graduates from high school but does so well prepared for the higher-education experience, and with the means to afford it. He is a former member of the board of directors of the National Association for College Admission Counseling, or NACAC, a membership organization of more than twenty-three thousand college admissions deans, counselors, and other professionals. In the fall of 2020, he was appointed to the board of the Lenfest Scholars Foundation. He has appeared periodically as a college admissions expert on NBC's *Today* show and, along with Eric, on the parenting website Grown & Flown.

The two of us also bring the perspective and empathy of having navigated this process ourselves as young people. And we're both parents, with children at various stages on the pathway between elementary school and a college degree. Eric has two children who are school age, while Jacques has recently had firsthand experience with the college process with his two children.

One reason we have titled this book *The College Conversation* is because it represents the continuation of an ongoing professional discussion that the two of us have been having for over a decade. This progressive and evolving dialogue began on *The Choice* blog of *The New York Times*—a free college admissions and financial aid resource that Jacques created in 2009 and led for the next four years, and on which Eric served as a regular guest expert. We've continued to discuss these issues in both public and private settings, including at conferences and on panels around the world.

We do want to acknowledge the roles each of us has played in occasionally fanning some of the trends in college admissions that could fairly be characterized as less constructive. Eric, for example, was among the many deans across the nation who release elaborate marketing materials each fall promoting the virtues of studying at his school, well aware that space in the incoming class is limited. Similarly, while presiding over *The Choice*, Jacques dutifully chronicled the ever-dwindling acceptance rates at the nation's most selective colleges and universities as if they were baseball scores, providing yet another forum for those institutions to compete head-to-head.

If your child is a high school student, they will soon be navigating a series of conversations of their own: with you; with representatives from prospective colleges; with their college counselor; and, perhaps most importantly, with themselves, looking inward to ask important questions with your guidance. Mindful of these interactions, we were struck (and moved) by an essay on another topic both personal and full of emotion that appeared in *The New York Times* in 2015 and went viral. Its title: "To Fall in Love with Anyone, Do This." That piece recounted the thirty-six questions that formed the basis for a study conducted more than twenty years ago by a psychologist who succeeded in making two subjects in his laboratory fall in love. They included "What would constitute a 'perfect' day for you?"

(Question 4); "If you could wake up tomorrow having gained any one quality or ability, what would it be?" (Question 12); "Your house, containing everything you own, catches fire. After saving your loved ones and pets, you have time to safely make a final dash to save any one item. What would it be? Why?" (Question 34).

Questions like these might not only be helpful in the admissions process (each could inspire a young person's thinking for a college essay) but could also encourage young people to think about themselves more deeply, and for more profound reasons than merely getting into college.

We've organized this book around five key discussions and themes, tracing the chronological arc of the admissions and financial aid process. We begin even before the assembly of a college list, with a section we call **Conversations About the Discovery Phase**, where we provide parents with prompts they might use to encourage their children to reflect on what they value and how they think. From there we dive into **Conversations About the Search**, which arms parents with a checklist of qualities and attributes against which their child might evaluate colleges and universities of interest. These are followed by **Conversations About the Application**, in which we break down each component of the application and provide tips on the college essay from our vantage points as professional writer and reader, and **Conversations About the Decisions**, which we define as the colleges' decisions, as well as your child's. We conclude with **Conversations About the Transition**, with our advice on helping your child thrive in the first year of college itself, including for those parents whose child may express an inclination to explore transferring to another institution.

Within each of those conversations is a series of more than a dozen activities designed to facilitate discussion, insight, and action plans. The tools you and your child will need to work through these activities can be as low-tech as an index card and Sharpie, or as elaborate as a Google Doc and spreadsheet. Where there's a keyword or concept that we wish to emphasize, we've tried to highlight it in bold, followed by a brief explanation.

At points throughout the book we have also expanded this conversation beyond ourselves and our backgrounds, so that we might enliven and amplify our discussion with a broader palette of best practices, expertise, and experience, as well voices from racial, ethnic, and socioeconomic backgrounds historically underrepresented on the nation's college and university campuses. To do so, we conducted some targeted joint reporting from the field, traveling, for example, to High Tech High, a small, innovative public charter high school on the site of an old navy base in San Diego. There we spoke to Larry Rosenstock, the school's founder; Chris White, its veteran college counselor; Jonathan Villafuerte, a college readiness consultant whose particular focus is first-generation students; and a handful of first-generation students and their parents. In Miami we interviewed Dr. Omar Monteagudo, the principal of the School for Advanced Studies, a pioneering public high school that partners with Miami Dade College.

To broaden our understanding of community college as well the process of transferring from community college to more traditional four-year institutions, we drew on our interviews with Alfred Herrera, an assistant vice provost at UCLA responsible for community college partnerships, and Mark Allen Poisel, a former senior administrator at the University of Central Florida who was most recently vice chancellor for student affairs at the University of Arkansas at Little Rock. We also met with Jenny Rickard, the president and chief executive officer of the Common Application, who formerly led admissions and enrollment at Bryn Mawr College and the University of Puget Sound, and Carol Sutton Lewis, the founder and chief executive officer of Ground Control Parenting, which provides information and advice tailored to parents of young people of color.

To enhance the portions of our conversation on college affordability, we sought out Charlie Javice, the founder and chief executive officer of Frank, a company that helps families navigate the financial aid process, with offerings that include a free platform that supports them in filing the FAFSA. And for advice about the transition from high school to college, we spent time with Harvey R. Fields Jr., associate dean for student success at Washington University in St. Louis. We quote many of these professionals directly in the pages that follow and learned much from all of them.

While readers will find no foolproof formula here to guarantee admission, we do seek to impart plenty of "news you can use." The admissions process is in many ways timeless, long governed by practitioners seeking to build a community of engaged students who might learn as much from one another as they do from their instructors. While elite colleges and universities attract more than enough qualified applicants to fill their first-year classes many times over, they nonetheless constantly seek to broaden and deepen their applicant pools. They do so, at least in part, because their competitors are engaged in a similar arms race; because, until 2018, *U.S. News & World Report* incorporated an institution's selectivity in the calculation of its annual rankings; because university boards of trustees pay as close attention to those rankings as students and parents do, if not more so; and because Standard & Poor's, which rates the financial stability of colleges and universities as if they were Fortune 500 companies, has taken a page from *U.S. News* and factors admission selectivity into those institutions' bond ratings.

For these reasons we also provide parents with some insights into the parallel conversations taking place within college admissions offices, so that they have a sense of the strategic objectives underpinning why, for example, a college may have phrased an essay question the way it did, or required a standardized test, and how its admissions office factors that information into its decision.

As we were completing the hardcover edition of this book in spring 2020, life in the nation and around the world—including on college and university campuses—was upended seemingly overnight by the spread of the novel coronavirus. As college and university students across the country were ordered to pack up their dorms, head home early, and finish their classes online, admissions committees labored to complete their selection of the following year's class. Some colleges and universities were soon weighing whether to begin the fall semester online, in person, or as a hybrid of both.

Admissions offices also canceled campus tours, including for admitted students seeking to finalize decisions of their own, as well as for high school sophomores and juniors beginning their college searches. As summer approached, and most of the nation's high school students remained confined to their homes, several administrations of the SAT and ACT were canceled, which, in turn, prompted most colleges and universities to make the tests optional, at least in the 2020–21 academic year. Among their concerns were those related to access and equity and the possibility that some students, particularly those from low-income backgrounds, would be shut out from taking the tests. With such exams no longer required—and with students struggling to cross colleges off their lists without opportunities for in-person due diligence—applications to many selective institutions soared. Meanwhile, other colleges struggled to fill their first-year classes. And, in a development that raised further concerns about access to higher education for low-income applicants in particular, the number of students who filled out the Free

Application for Federal Student Aid dropped by nearly 10 percent. Every high school student was impacted in some way, whether academically or in their activities and social lives.

As we were completing the paperback edition of *The College Conversation* in spring 2021, the increasingly widespread availability of vaccinations was offering hope of a return to in-person classes and other activities for many colleges and universities—as well as, where travel and other local restrictions permit, the resumption of campus visits. As all this was unfolding in real time in ways that once seemed unimaginable, it served as a reminder that any plans you establish through the College Conversation must have a degree of flexibility, and even contingency, particularly when situations arise outside your control. And yet the bedrock principles underpinning the admissions process, and the conversations we encourage families to have as part of them, remain as relevant as ever—perhaps even more so in these most uncertain times.

We want to close by acknowledging that even under the most ideal conditions, we're highly conscious of how pressed you as parents are for time at such a busy and stressful juncture in your children's lives. In the pages that follow, we've tried not to overstay our welcome and to lead you through this process in ways that are thoughtful, focused, and purposeful.

Preface

As readers of this book you may be joining the College Conversation at different points in your child's development. But our particular focus here will be for parents of children currently in middle school or high school. If your oldest child is still in elementary school, our strong counsel is to let them enjoy being children—exploring their academic interests and having fun—as you gain insight into their emerging learning styles.

For those of you whose children are in middle school—typically grades six through eight—we believe that these years are far too early in a child's development to be visiting colleges, and we can assure you that no college admissions officer is going to be dipping into your child's middle school record as part of an admission decision. But the course selection that you and your child make in the middle school years can impact later academic choices. For example, a pre-algebra course in eighth grade can serve as a foundation for more advanced math classes in high school. You as a parent also have to balance whatever advice you do offer with your knowledge of your child and the importance of not pushing them too hard too early.

The same is true of extracurricular activities. As children approach their early teens, these should be a source of enjoyment, as well as enhancing their physical fitness and well-being. Let them explore a wide range of activities that might help them discover what they like and who they are. Middle school parents should not be looking ahead to senior year of high school, when their children will be dutifully listing their many extracurricular activities in their college applications. At a certain point during the transition from middle school to high school, their sampling may come to an end and their interests into sharper focus, as their lives become more complicated and busy with the demands of high school and adolescence. At this point they're going to need you to provide some guidance and structure to help inform their decisions regarding those activities on which they might focus.

Middle school is also a time in children's lives when they begin to develop the habits and pursuits that can serve them well in their high school and college years. Here we are talking about the child who makes a habit of reading for pleasure at night or whose interest in something like baseball box scores or the beam in gymnastics begins to cross the line to passion. Don't push them to develop these habits and have these experiences with an end result in mind, but rather for the joy of doing so.

For those whose children are about to make the transition into ninth grade, please don't view this moment as the firing of a starter pistol signaling a mad race to cram your child's life with so many advanced courses, near-perfect grades, and pursuits outside the classroom that sleep becomes a rare luxury.

Now we know what you might be thinking: only a few pages ago we noted that in spring 2020 the University of Pennsylvania offered admission to only 8 percent of an applicant pool of more than 42,000, almost enough to fill Franklin Field, the school's football stadium. Surely those teenagers fortunate enough to have been offered a space in the class shared one quality in common: perfection in every demonstrable category, having been ridden hard by parents who had somehow decoded the secret formula for acceptance.

Not even close.

Aside from the fact that there *is* no such formula—you are going to have to trust us both on that—this is your opportunity as a parent to set a tone that will encourage your child to value the four years of high school as its own experience, rather than as merely a means to an end. And it's also your chance to disabuse them of the notion that there is any such thing as "perfect" when it comes to college admission. Later in this book we'll explain that a good and effective college application is in fact a natural summation of these years, capturing lessons learned and experiences had, ideally for the sheer pleasure of those moments. If, on the other hand, you communicate to your child, however indirectly, that you view high school as one giant résumé builder, you will likely set them up for two disappointments. The first: they might not get into their chosen school. But the second disappointment is far more tragic: they will have missed out on the opportunity to make their own choices, develop their own interests, and, quite possibly, enjoy the journey of learning itself.

Which is not to say that the high school years—and decisions made about courses, and how your children spend their time—aren't critically important. But by placing those years in the proper perspective for your children at the outset, you (and they) will be in a better position to find fulfillment, while also preparing them (and you) as they set sail on one of the many routes to and through college.

To get started with the approach we offer in this book, you might divide your child's high school experience into eight segments—basically carving each year into two parts. One reason we suggest you do so is that you, as a parent, are likely to find these shorter intervals to be more manageable, like a runner seeing a marathon not as twenty-six miles but as a sequence of stages. This framing might also help your child to view the school year not as an interminable, 180-day stretch—where a stumble or rough patch might leave them fearing they will never recover—but as a continuum of segments in which they are alternating periods of high intensity with, ideally, rest, renewal, and reflection.

As Jonathan Villafuerte, the college consultant at High Tech High in San Diego, put it to us, "You're not going to wake up one day and say, 'OK, I'm going to conquer the world.' But you can wake up one day and say, 'I'm going to conquer this day.'" He added, "And by taking small steps in the right direction, the results will be visible in the long term."

To help you chart these cycles, while being careful not to take on your child's workload as your own, consult a copy of your child's high school's academic calendar and note key dates—including exam periods, parent-teacher conferences, and breaks—on your own calendar. You may have already been doing this for years, but do so now with a different purpose: to make yourself aware of those short intervals where exertion gives way to recovery.

In the pages that follow, you may find at first that we can be a bit top-heavy with advice for parents of children who may be aiming for some of the nation's more selective institutions of higher education. We offer this information in part to ensure that they are intentional about taking the courses that could serve to lay the foundation to preserve such options. While most of the nation's colleges and universities don't necessarily require that applicants take the most rigorous curriculum available at their high schools, they do expect students to challenge themselves—not only for the experience of growing and learning, but also for preparation to do college-level work. If your child is among the many who are not interested in the nation's most selective colleges and universities, rest assured that we will soon broaden our perspective to encompass a full range of higher-education options, both four-year and two-year.

In dividing high school into eight segments, natural pauses will occur between each, including stretches of respite in the winter and summer. Avoid the temptation to overprogram your child during these periods, and instead give them space and license to decompress. We're not endorsing indulging in extended laziness (or time on the Xbox), but we do recognize that these are also times when your children may need to work a part-time job or take care of family responsibilities.

If you are picking up this book at the outset of your child's entry into high school, be aware of the many choices and possibilities that lie before them. At thirteen or fourteen years old, they may have already defined themselves, whether as a STEM kid interested in science, technology, engineering, or math; or an arts buff; or a jock (or found that they're starting to be labeled as such). We hope you'll encourage them to be open to revising or even rewriting these assumptions. At this stage, they'll be dealing with a great deal of change in their lives, including navigating new spaces and relationships. Give them the opportunity to settle in and learn more about themselves without having to know what their next step should be.

When we talk about academic choices and possibilities, understand there is wide variance in high school offerings and resources across the nation (context that admissions officers understand and take into account in their review) and that one size most certainly does not fit all.

Some choices in high school may have already been made for

your child, such as the sequence offered in math or science. For example, in mathematics, a traditional five-year sequence (perhaps beginning in middle school) might progress in the following order: algebra 1, geometry, algebra 2/trigonometry, pre-calculus, and calculus. If your child is going to be able to take some level of calculus in their senior year of high school (a necessary foundational course for engineering and business in college), then they would need to take algebra 1 in eighth grade. Otherwise your child may choose to accelerate their math studies in high school, such as by taking a summer course. In some high schools across the country, and certainly around the world, students have further accelerated into more advanced mathematics, including multivariable calculus and linear algebra. Please note, however, that the number of students embarking on such a course represents just a sliver of the universe.

In science, the traditional high school curriculum sequence is biology, chemistry, and physics, followed by an advanced level of these courses or an elective in areas like computer science or environmental science. Prospective engineering applicants might consider taking the next level of physics, not only to be a competitive applicant, but also to have the strongest foundation upon which to build later. Finally, some high schools have adopted the Physics First curriculum of the American Association of Physics Teachers, in which students enroll in a physics class in ninth grade, rather than biology. Parents whose children have access to that curriculum, and who are considering taking it, should bear in mind that critics have raised concerns that some children don't have sufficient grounding in math to take on physics that early.

As their high school years progress, students' options (including for taking electives) will increase. But even within the fairly proscribed ninth- and tenth-grade years, there are decisions to be made.

Should, for example, a course be taken at a certain level, such as an honors or advanced?

A word of caution, and perhaps reassurance: admissions officers at highly selective institutions will often cite their preference for considering students who have taken the most rigorous curriculum available at their high school. Some students will naturally choose to max out their course choices in just this way, with a minimal level of stress. But admissions officers also recognize that many other students—perhaps a majority—who are aiming for highly selective institutions in particular will start to feel quite a bit of strain after taking perhaps three advanced courses. Indeed, there is at this very moment a backlash not only among parents and counselors but within the admissions field, recognizing that students have been pushed too hard in recent years at the expense of learning and well-being.

Which is not to say that admissions officers are advocating that your child take it easy during their high school years. Whatever courses they choose, they need to challenge themselves, put in the effort, and strive to do the best they can. Many students will opt for a high school curriculum with no advanced classes. To them (and their parents), we'll echo a point we made in the introduction to this book: the higher-education landscape is vast, with quite literally thousands of options for a postsecondary experience that will align with a student's interests and readiness.

For parents of children who aspire to attend one of the fifty or so most selective institutions in the nation, you might use the following as a guide for a complete high school curriculum: four years each of English, of a single foreign language (an eighth-grade class may well count toward this, perhaps the only circumstance in which a middle school course is considered), and of math and science, along with three years of history and social science. (The eight private colleges and universities of the Ivy League are actually quite explicit about these requirements on their website.) In addition, you should periodically check in with your child to ensure that across their curriculum they are honing their writing and other communication skills and that they are seeking resources and support from their teachers and other mentors (including after school) in these areas. Eric's perspective on the importance of these skills comes, in large part, from reading thousands of submissions from seventeen- and eighteen-year-old writers each year and coming away astonished at the weaknesses in their writing. That concern is echoed by many college faculty, including in the sciences, who lament the various ways in which their students' insufficient readiness for college writing holds them back.

As a professional writer for more than a quarter century, Jacques's counsel to parents is fairly straightforward: for an aspiring writer, there is no substitute for practice, whether composing essays or term papers, or even writing in a daily journal that is for your child's eyes only. He also suggests that when your child is given a range of length for a writing assignment by a teacher, they might consider aiming for the middle or upper end of that range, as opposed to the bare minimum—while avoiding padding their prose for the sheer purpose of hitting a targeted word count.

Just as your child will need to make a series of academic choices in high school, they will also need to make tough decisions about how they wish to spend their time outside the classroom. Those decisions should be guided by the experiences themselves. You might help your child frame their extracurricular activities in three categories. First are those pursuits in which they truly excel and are seen as leaders—the kid who more often than not is given the basketball with seconds on the clock, or who is assigned the lead story in the newspaper. A second category is for those endeavors they engage in for the sheer joy of participation, with no expectation that they are the go-to person—the rank-and-file member of the chorus, as op-posed to the soloist. Our final category is a bit of a catchall, encom-passing those many weekly opportunities to step away for reflection and for contribution to one's family and community. These moments could take place through local service projects, religious observance, or being able to have a family meal without distractions.

The three basic categories in our out-of-classroom rubric also happen to align with the priorities of the admissions process, includ-ing at highly selective institutions. We'll go a bit deeper into this later, but suffice it to say that, because they are eager to build com-munities on their campuses, colleges want to have a sense of how your children will interact and engage with peers and faculty, as well as of the various strengths and passions they bring. Some students will be more rounded, others more specialized.

For those reading this book at a moment when the aftereffects of the pandemic are still making it challenging to engage in some activities—or who may be lamenting all the time lost—we wish to express two thoughts. First, as parents ourselves, we can appreciate how your child must be feeling. Second, so, too, will the college ad-missions offices.

And with that, we're going to move beyond the walls of your child's high school as we begin the part of the College Conversation we call Discovery.

PART I

---

*Conversations About
the Discovery Phase*

(A.) The "Why College?" Conversation

These are most certainly days of disruption in higher education. At some private four-year colleges and universities, the full cost of attendance (before financial aid) can approach $80,000. That figure is not only well above the median family income in this country ($63,179, according to the U.S. Census Bureau) but it has increased at rates far higher than inflation at many points over the last few decades. At prices this high, families are wise to consider the return on such an investment, including its usefulness as preparation for entering the workforce and a career.

We believe that there is still a strong case to be made for acquiring a traditional four-year bachelor's degree, beyond its utilitarian value, though with a few caveats. Once again, you need to know your child—and to ask them, and yourself, some fundamental questions. Do you, as a parent, feel that as the end of their senior year of high school approaches, they are emotionally ready for a four-year college experience, whether living at home or independently on campus?

Even with the range of price points for four-year college tuition (whether at an in-state public institution, which is typically more reasonably priced, or at a private institution that offers deep discounts in the form of financial aid), is a bachelor's degree something that you as a family can afford?

There is also the question of the goal and purpose of your child's attending a four-year institution. Are they interested, for example, in the intrinsic value of learning and knowledge? Of having opportunities to build relationships and to network? And to what extent do they see college as a pathway to a career, or at least as laying the groundwork for it? Finally, does your child view college, at least in part, as preparation for a graduate school experience, including medical school, law school, or other professional degree?

In this section we hope to provide you with some supporting evidence for the importance of a four-year degree and a return on that investment. But we'll also consider other paths—including associate's degrees, the transfer process between community college and more traditional four-year colleges, and career credentialing. In some ways the range of such educational choices following high school is unique to the United States, where one doesn't have to decide on a career at eighteen years old.

When we refer to "discovery" in the title of this chapter, we're imagining conversations in which your child will discover aspects of themselves that will help guide them through this process and will serve not only to enlighten them but you as a parent, too. Before we get started, let's define a few basic terms.

Bachelor's Degree

A strong body of evidence exists that supports the value of studying for and completing a bachelor's degree. In terms of lifetime earnings, the latest figures from the Bureau of Labor Statistics reveal that people who attain at least a bachelor's degree will earn roughly $2.4 million over their lifetime—about $1 million more than someone whose education did not advance beyond a high school degree and $600,000 more than those with an associate's degree. Meanwhile, that bachelor's is an essential gateway to a master's degree ($2.8 million in lifetime earnings) and a professional degree ($4.2 million).

Omar Monteagudo, the principal of the School for Advanced Studies in Miami, a partnership between the Miami Dade County Public Schools and Miami Dade College, tells students as well as parents, "The bachelor's degree is what the high school diploma used to be ten, twenty, thirty years ago."

Jennifer Delahunty, the former dean of admissions of Kenyon College in Ohio, is the editor of a book with a title intended as a not-so-subtle rebuke from children to their parents—*I'm Going to College—Not You!* It includes an essay by Gail Hudson, a writer based in Seattle, who advises families to broaden the concept of the return on investment of a bachelor's degree beyond just dollars and cents. "More income doesn't necessarily mean more happiness," she writes. "Education can't buy us loving spouses and joyful lives."

If a bachelor's-degree-granting institution, particularly one rooted in the liberal arts, is doing its job well, then its graduates will develop critical-thinking skills and the ability to communicate clearly and persuasively. These are skills and qualities that can ultimately benefit the larger community and are essential to the functioning of a democratic society.

For young people who may be the first in their families to attend college—or those whose family income ranks among the lowest in the nation—there is also persuasive research demonstrating the value of a bachelor's degree as a vehicle for social mobility. For example, children from low-income families who graduate from the nation's most selective colleges have nearly the same odds of reaching the top fifth of the nation's income distribution as their peers from higher-income families, according to a study by the Equality of Opportunity Project.

"A college education acts as a leveler, dramatically reducing the correlation between parents' income and the adult incomes of their children," the researchers Richard V. Reeves and Eleanor Krause wrote in a Brookings Institution blog post in January 2018. "This is true for elite colleges, other four-year institutions, and community colleges."

Enrolling in a bachelor's-degree-granting institution should not be assumed to be a guarantee of completion. Studies have shown that as many as 40 percent of young people who enroll in a four-year college or university don't go on to graduate from that institution. While some will transfer to other schools and complete their degrees there, many others will drop out as a result of not being properly prepared for college work and the college experience, or being swamped in debt, to say nothing of being distracted by hours spent working a part-time job to defray the cost of that education.

Associate's Degree

There are many reasons—and arguably more today than ever before—why your child might want to at least consider beginning their education after high school at a community college. Parents and young people alike would do well to bear in mind what Alfred Herrera, an assistant vice provost at UCLA, told us: "Community college *is* college."

A big argument for community college is economic. While many families hesitate to commit to the cost of a traditional four-year college degree, an associate's program can be a much more economical option. For example, a year spent as a full-time student in an associate's program at a community college will have an annual average cost of less than $4,000. That compares to roughly $40,000, on average, for tuition for a year of full-time study at a four-year private college or university.

In an ideal world some, if not all, community college credits would be transferable to a four-year institution—enabling your child to save no small amount on the first year or two of tuition while still graduating with a bachelor's degree. The State University System of Florida and the California State University system are among many across the country that have so-called **articulation agreements** that formalize the transfer of associate's credits to bachelor's programs. A student who successfully completes an associate's degree at one of 115 California community colleges is guaranteed priority admission to at least one college in its state university system, though not necessarily to the campus of their choice. (The program even has the catchy name "Degree with a Guarantee.") As another example, the State University of New York at New Paltz has agreements governing transfer credits with more than three hundred community colleges.

"We're not suggesting students stop at an associate's degree," Dr. Herrera, who also leads the Academic Advancement Program at UCLA, explained. "The whole idea is to get job training or to go the transfer route."

We want to emphasize, however, that despite the many opportunities available to transfer associate's degree credits to bachelor's degree programs, many four-year colleges do not accept such credits, or may have strict rules for doing so. Your child should be sure to check with the relevant institutions early in the process about how such credits will be handled.

Another reason your child might consider starting their postsecondary education at a community college is more emotional in nature, and perhaps related to maturity as well as burnout. Your child might also feel that they are not quite ready to make the commitment, emotional or otherwise, to enrolling at a four-year school, which could include living independently. Although parents might be inclined to advise their children to power through to a four-year setting straight from high school, community college can offer something of a modest respite close to home. Attending a local community college might also enable your child to better tend to important domestic responsibilities, such as caring for an ill family member or working to help support the household—obligations that might not leave a student much of a choice in the school they attend. Of course, as an alternative, many nearby four-year colleges and universities that would enable students to live at home could also help satisfy all these objectives.

If your child is considering beginning their education at a community college, establish a purposeful plan for doing so. According to the National Student Clearinghouse Research Center, only 13 percent of community college students went on to earn a bachelor's degree within six years. For at least some of those who did not, an associate's degree may, in fact, be the most appropriate way to complete a formal postsecondary education. A bachelor's is not for everyone, and depending on your child's career goals, it may not even be necessary.

There may also be opportunities for your child to take community college courses for credit while still in high school. These dual enrollment programs have sprouted up at high schools and community colleges around the nation to offer high school students access to a more rigorous curriculum. Courses in dual enrollment programs can serve as a supplement to those offered within a traditional high school setting, including through the College Board's Advanced Placement program. By enrolling in these courses, students demonstrate their initiative and intellectual inquisitiveness, as well as their desire to seek out a challenge.

Aligning Military Service with a College Degree

Parents whose children are interested in military service should be aware that it does not foreclose the pursuit of a college degree. In the wake of the conflicts in Afghanistan and Iraq, many colleges and universities have established admissions initiatives specifically aimed at veterans. Under the Post-9/11 GI Bill and its associated Yellow Ribbon Program, veterans who served on or after September 11, 2001, are eligible for financial support from the federal government to defray the cost of at least a portion of their higher-education expenses. More information can be found in the benefits section on the U.S. Department of Veterans Affairs website.

Students who wish to serve in the military while attending college have the option of joining the Reserve Officers' Training Corps (ROTC), which is currently available at more than 1,700 colleges and universities across the nation in partnership with all branches of the military. Students enrolled in ROTC have the cost of their college tuition partially (and in some cases fully) funded by the military and the opportunity to earn the rank of officer, in exchange for a commitment to serve in an active-duty capacity for at least three years upon graduation.

At the University of Pennsylvania, where there is a Navy ROTC program, Eric worked directly with a navy liaison who identifies candidates in the university's admissions pool who have been awarded NROTC scholarships. He personally reviewed every application from an NROTC candidate, which students submit through a separate process that runs parallel to the traditional admissions system.

Another option is one of the nation's five service academies, which were established "for the undergraduate education and training of commissioned officers for the United States Armed Forces." In the order of their founding, they are: the U.S. Military Academy in West Point, New York; the Naval Academy in Annapolis, Maryland; the Coast Guard Academy in New London, Connecticut; the Merchant Marine Academy in Kings Point, New York; and the Air Force Academy in Colorado Springs, Colorado. In addition to having the cost of their tuition and room and board covered by the U.S. government, and earning the rank of officer, graduates of the five service academies are also awarded bachelor of science degrees. As is the case with recipients of ROTC scholarships, graduates of the service academies commit to active-duty service. Candidates for admission must apply directly to each academy and secure a nomination typically from a member of Congress (or a delegate, in the case of residents of the District of Columbia and Puerto Rico). Applicants must also pass a rigorous physical exam.

Alternate Paths to a College Degree or Other Postsecondary Credential

One of the relatively new forms of education is massive open online courses (MOOCs). These may be available for free, but there is typically a nominal charge for those who wish to earn a certificate of completion. In some instances it is possible to earn an associate's, bachelor's, or even master's degree entirely online, at a fraction of the cost of an on-campus, brick-and-mortar experience. And as with dual enrollment programs, an increasing number of high school students are supplementing their education—including in areas like calculus, advanced writing, and computer coding—by accessing these curricula online. Coursera offers more than 3,600 courses and is affiliated with nearly two hundred colleges and universities. Companies like Amazon and Cisco also offer Coursera courses, for employees as well as the general public.

For a variety of reasons, none of the credentials discussed in this section may be of interest to—or appropriate for—many learners, including those who may wish to go directly from high school into a trade. Parents seeking information about industry-approved credentials available on that pathway might begin by logging on to the website of an institution like Lincoln Tech. Its CEO, Scott M. Shaw, describes the mission of the institution, which was founded in 1946, as "training students for in-demand careers in some of America's most important industries," ranging from diesel technology to medical billing, and from culinary arts to welding.

Some parents will remain unpersuaded about the value of a college education altogether and will wish to steer their children clear of one—at least initially. Currently only a little more than a third of American adults have a bachelor's degree or higher. A movement called UnCollege promoting alternatives to higher education was founded by Dale J. Stephens. Homeschooled as a child, Stephens dropped out of Hendrix College in Arkansas to accept a $100,000 fellowship from Peter Thiel, the cofounder of PayPal. Stephens used his fellowship to create UnCollege, which provides "resources for self-directed learning, dropping out of college, and hacking your education," with a vision of "a world where people take ownership of their education." Stephens prizes the acquisition of skills and the value of real-world experiences. Visitors to the UnCollege website can also find downloadable guides on subjects like "Should I Drop Out of College?" and "Ten Crucial Skills They Won't Teach You in School."

But even the UnCollege movement has recently begun to come around, at least in part, to the merits of a college education for some students. It also offers a "Year On" program, a formal gap-year break beginning as early as the sophomore year of high school, set in Indonesia, Mexico, Peru, and Tanzania, among other locales. UnCollege makes the case that students who take a gap year "are more likely to graduate than their peers, experience higher job satisfaction, and perform better in their first year at college."

(B.) Helping Your Child Imagine Their (Ideal) College Campus

ACTIVITY #1: Jotting Down a Few Key Attributes on an Index Card

Now that we've outlined the range of basic levels of American higher education, it's time for you and your child to begin the process of looking inward at the specific attributes of a college or university experience and environment that might have the most appeal.

For this first exercise, you and your child should grab a few index cards and sit apart from each other, with the expectation that you will come back together to compare notes and to see where your respective visions for the ideal college experience align and diverge. Assuming your child is game, provide them with a series of instructions drawn from the suggestions that follow but adapted for your child's own personality and priorities. Remind them that their card should reflect *their* ideas and acknowledge that the college experience is ultimately theirs, not yours. If despite your prodding they're resistant, this will still be a worthy process for you to engage in alone, or perhaps with a spouse or other partner, as it will provide you with valuable insights into your own thinking, with the possibility that you may be able to coax your child to the table at another time.

On your card, spend a few minutes writing a handful of words and phrases that describe the college environment that you believe might best suit your child. Don't cite the names of individual schools or describe a school in a way that is so specific that its identity is obvious. There will be opportunities later in your extended conversation for you to share with your child particular institutions that you feel could be a good fit.

What we're advocating here as a starting point is reducing the college experience to its barest essentials. Is there a particular subject (or subjects) that your child might enjoy studying? How about a particular setting—rural, urban, or something in between? Is athletics, varsity or intramural, a priority?

You might also consider a few attributes that are less tangible: Do you see your child as thriving in a college environment with a lot of energy, which could be inherent in the size of the institution, such as on a big football Saturday? Or will your child thrive in a less frenzied setting, as is typical on a smaller campus? Be aware that there are many schools that fall between these extremes, and that your child could well thrive in a range of environments.

Finally, identify any aspects of the college process that could be a source of anxiety. For example, if you have concerns about your child's prospects for admission, particularly at a highly selective institution, as well as your family's ability to pay for that education, include that.

The point of this exercise is to lay the groundwork for a mature conversation that may involve some discomfort but provide a beneficial amount of transparency.

At this initial stage, don't overthink things. Free-associate a bit, with the goal of coming up with a half dozen partially formed ideas. This is the roughest of rough drafts, and it will undergo any number of rewrites over time. But keep these cards close by, to the point that they become dog-eared as you test your initial assumptions throughout all phases of the College Conversation.

For those who are doing this exercise on the earlier side of the admissions process, such as during your child's sophomore year of high school, take a broader, more flexible approach, as you'll be refining your initial thoughts multiple times over the next few years. But if it's the fall of your child's senior year of high school, by necessity you'll have to be more focused and precise, as time is now of the essence.

For the purposes of this discussion, let's assume your child has been willing to play along with the exercise. After you've each retreated to your respective corners for five minutes or so, come back together, exchange cards, and spend some time reviewing and reflecting on what the other has written. If both parents or another adult is involved, this could be a three-way exchange.

A good way to begin a dialogue is by identifying areas in which you concur, such as if you both agree that an optimal distance from home ranges from a one-hour to a four-hour drive. But what about those topics where you and your child are not in agreement, whether it's an intended major or an anxiety you or they have? This is not the time to craft solutions or seek to forge common ground, as the mere raising of these issues—perhaps for the first time in your relationship—is the objective at this point. Take note of each other's thinking—the goal at this early stage is simply to notice, to listen, and to begin to learn.

Be mindful of topics that might trigger strong emotions, whether yours or your child's. Your preference may be for a campus less than a few hours' drive from home, while your child dreams of being a continent away. Take note of your child's body language and expressions. If they are retreating inward or obviously anxious, don't press the issue but reassure them that discomfort in such discussions is natural, and essential to growth, and that you are in this together. Before you bring your conversation to a close, highlight for your child the various points that you'll be likely to return to in future talks, as they'll become more important as your child begins to assemble a college list and then sets out to learn more about these institutions.

c. Rules of the Road: Establishing Guardrails for Your Role as a Parent

As you discuss the activity on the previous pages with your child, you may gain some fresh insights into the degree to which they wish to engage with you on such an emotionally fraught subject and their openness to doing so. Layered onto this conversation are the nearly two decades of interactions you have had on any number of subjects, each registering at various levels on your family's emotional thermometer and governed by long-established rules of engagement.

In that context, view the College Conversation in your home as one more subject for discussion, albeit one involving no small amount of complexity and raw emotion. Because it's hardly the only conversation taking place in your family, and because the regular rhythms of life must continue, develop a plan for talking about college in ways that don't overwhelm everyone, while still ensuring the conditions for your child's success.

Work with your child (and your partner or spouse, as appropriate) to establish some basic guardrails and boundaries that will govern how and when you engage in the College Conversation, as well as when you should take a breather. If another adult is taking part in the conversation, you both might establish your own rules of engagement. Whether that person is a spouse (married or divorced), stepparent, grandparent, or family friend, spend some time thinking about how you will work together in support of your child. This may involve setting up a division of labor—is one of you, for example, more comfortable with research or logistics? You should also agree upon ways of managing the differences and disagreements that are inevitable in a process like this. To the extent that you and another adult have different points of view, you might want to consider how to convey them to your child in the most constructive way.

We consider these broader rules of the road important enough that it is probably worth your writing them down or tapping them into a computer so that they can serve as a reference.

Stacks of parenting books have been written about the wide range of styles that exists between permissive parenting and authoritarian parenting, with those parents who strive to be firm but warm falling somewhere in between. One book that that we have found informative is *The Stressed Years of Their Lives: Helping Your Kid Survive and Thrive During Their College Years* (2019) by B. Janet Hibbs and Anthony Rostain. To the extent you have not done so already, have a conversation with your child about the appropriate balance of your involvement as a parent in their college process. Because no two families are the same, there is no one-size-fits-all formula we can provide here, so we urge you to reach an understanding with your child about what you both believe will work best in terms of your role as a parent.

As you do so, keep in mind the advice shared with us by Chris White, the longtime college counselor at High Tech High in San Diego, who said that the common denominator among those students who have had a successful college process over the years has been an engaged parent, regardless of their own education. White avoids, however, equating parental involvement and engagement with the much-maligned conception of helicopter parenting.

Our own advice is that you consider discussing with your child where they need you to provide scaffolding and other support and where you believe they would benefit from that reinforcement, as well as where they would prefer that you step back and allow them the room to make some of their own decisions.

There is probably no more important advice we can provide here than a basic reminder to take the time to really hear your child. "Parents have to listen to their kids," said Monica Mendez, a pharmacy technician and the parent of two first-generation students who graduated from High Tech High and enrolled at Gettysburg College in Pennsylvania. Her husband, Armando, a barber on a naval base in San Diego, amended that to say, "You need to be able to listen without judgment." Or, we as practitioners might respectfully add, without *rushing* to judgment.

Ariana Campos, another first-generation student at High Tech High, who enrolled at the George Washington University in Washington, DC, in the fall of 2019, emphasized the importance of parents keeping an open mind—even if they didn't initially agree with a point their child made. "It can be hurtful to just be shut down," she told us.

"Listen to me," she recalls saying to her mother. "This is something I'm passionate about."

Let's return to the construction of setting guardrails and boundaries, beginning with the question of "When?"

When in the course of your day-to-day family life, in a typical week, do you want to set aside time to talk about the college process? It could be a family dinner on a particular night, such as a Sunday—but depending on your child and family dynamic, discussing college during dinnertime (especially during that rare night when the stars align and you all eat together as a family) could make that meal a bit fraught. Perhaps a walk or an extended car ride would be more suitable, or a conversation over a therapeutic late evening dessert. You will know best when and where to engage—and when and where your child might feel most comfortable.

Some timing, though, may be out of your hands. Decisions will have to be made around deadlines, whether for standardized tests or financial aid or application submissions. If your child is fortunate to attend a high school with a strong college counseling office, its staff will be scheduling conversations with both your child and you at key milestones along the college pathway. These can serve to provide a timetable of when to begin this conversation with your child in earnest.

In families where there is more than one child, particularly children who are younger, we encourage you to be mindful of when it might be appropriate for them to be present at points in the College Conversation, as well as other times when it might be best for there to be some separation. A lot will depend on the age and maturity of those other children, as well as their dynamics with the child who is applying to college. Communication is key. Be sure to proactively consult all involved and to listen. The child who is actually applying should get a bit more say about how and whether to involve siblings in these discussions, and on outings like college tours.

You should also establish with your child parameters for what you and they will discuss about the admissions process outside of your own family. If your child wishes to keep their thinking and deliberations private, respect that desire. When a neighbor, however well intended, asks you a series of probing questions about your child's college plans, feel free to respond with a polite demurral, letting them know that the process is personal and that you are following your child's lead.

On the other hand, parents and families who have gone through this process in years past can be an enormous source of information, guidance, and support, particularly if you are a parent who has not had firsthand experience with college or the college application process. Take what they say judiciously—fact-checking where necessary, and cognizant that no two children are the same. Just be sure to be open with your child, informing them that you are embarking on these other conversations, while bearing in mind any ground rules they might have for you.

You and your child might also establish some ground rules for how you are going to discuss some of the most anxiety-producing elements of this process, without its dominating every interaction you have. What we don't want you to do is to practice avoidance of difficult or uncomfortable conversations. Pull back and look within yourself a bit to understand your own concerns, fears, and anxieties and how they might be impacting your conversations with your child. Carol Sutton Lewis, the parenting expert quoted earlier, suggests that you consider seeking out another adult—it could be a parent who has gone through this process with another child, a college counselor, or, depending on the issue, a licensed clinical therapist—to discuss your emotions. With the benefit of the insight they can offer, you might find yourself in a better position to consider whether or how to express your concerns to your child, such as worries you might be having about college affordability, or your child's forthcoming departure from home, or your own hopes and dreams about what specific school they might want to attend.

We want to close this section with a word of caution against you or your child living this phase of the college process online. Or, to put it another way, your child's college tour may be the one family vacation that you don't want to share widely on Facebook or Instagram. A seemingly innocuous photo of your child beaming in front of the founder's statue at a particular school could telegraph more to your friends and family than is appropriate, particularly during the early days of the search. As we all have learned, those photos have a permanent life on the internet, which can create additional anxieties down the road, as applications are submitted (or not) and decisions are rendered.

We also want to make a broader point about what your child, or you for that matter, shares on social media or even in a text message or Google Doc that was intended to be private. Any such material can be considered fair game, as far as the colleges are concerned, in the event that something inflammatory your child has written is brought to the attention of a college admissions officer. Remember that colleges are seeking to assemble communities, and they make judgments on what sort of citizen of that community your child will be. What your child says on social media can also jeopardize the status of their admission decision.

Most college acceptance letters will include the caveat that admission is contingent on the applicant's maintaining their academic standing, as well as their standing within their communities. For example, the acceptance letter sent by Harvard in the spring of 2019 to incoming first-year students included a warning that the university "reserves the right to withdraw an offer of admission under various conditions, including 'if you engage or have engaged in behavior that brings into question your honesty, maturity, or moral character.'" Harvard cited this very sentence in rescinding admission to an applicant from Marjory Stoneman Douglas High School in Parkland, Florida, who had been found to have written a series of "derogatory and racist screeds," as The New York Times put it, referencing an announcement the student himself made on Twitter. Two years earlier, CNN, among other news outlets, reported that at least ten incoming Harvard freshmen had their acceptances withdrawn after university administrators discovered they had been sharing "explicit memes" in a Facebook chat group.

Without necessarily scaring your child, it is your responsibility as parents to encourage them to be judicious about everything they post, regardless of whether it has any overt connection to the college process. Occasionally an online comment that winds up sinking a candidacy is brought to a college's attention by an outsider, well-meaning or otherwise. Use the college process as a teaching moment with your child about how much to share about themselves, and with whom.

(D.) Around the Kitchen Table: Preparing Parents to Help Children Get to Know Themselves

Now that you've established a basic framework for how to talk with your child about the admissions process, consider leveraging that newfound capital to encourage some deeper self-reflection on your child's part. You may know that your child is unique, but this is a moment for them to gain insight into who they are. They can't really know where they want to go to college without first figuring that out. What do they value? What motivates them? What do they seek out in friendships, in life experiences? What choices and decisions have they made, up until this point, in terms of how they spend their time?

While it's a valuable exercise at any stage of life—indeed, a parent contemplating a change of career might benefit from engaging in it—this particular activity will yield dividends for your child throughout the college application process. Some of the questions posed above are the very ones that the colleges themselves will ask. Your child's self-reflections will also inform their application essays, as well as guide their way to the teachers whom they will ask to write recommendations on their behalf.

When Eric speaks in front of parent audiences, he has framed this self-reflection exercise as the "Five I's."

ACTIVITY #2: The Five I's

Unlike the index card exercise on attributes in Activity #1, this is primarily an activity for your child to engage in, with you, as a parent, facilitating as you and they see fit.

In this instance, your child will need a larger card or a legal pad, or a Word or Google Doc. They will probably also want to have their index card handy as they embark on this next leg of their journey.

Over the course of forty-five minutes or so, have your child respond to the following five prompts, all of which begin with the letter "I": **identity, intellect, ideas, interests,** and **inspiration**.

Let's take a moment and provide a brief description of each.

Identity: How do you see yourself, and how do others see you?

Intellect: How do you approach the acquisition of knowledge? Do you delight in the challenge of doing research and lose track of time while reading?

Ideas: What do you think about, and what are some of the opinions you hold most dear?

Interests: What do you like to do with your free time?

Inspiration: What really motivates and moves you, and whom do you admire?

We made the point earlier that this harvesting of knowledge about one's self can help inform the selection of the two high school teachers who will write recommendations on your child's behalf. That selection, in turn, can help refine the personal narrative that your child will develop in other parts of the application. It's worth noting that those two recommendations can each highlight different aspects of your child's academic identity. For example, an Advanced Placement history teacher could attest to self-motivation, engagement in classroom conversation, and writing ability, particularly for a student who might be interested in majoring in that subject. A second recommendation could come from a teacher who could provide valuable insight into and context for your child's work ethic and motivation, perhaps in completing tasks that don't come to them as naturally. Another possibility for a second recommendation could be from a teacher in a course in which your child registered the lowest grade on their transcript, even if it's a C, if that teacher could provide supporting testimony as to your child's persistence when confronting academic obstacles.

We'll have more to say about teacher recommendations in the Application section of this book, but our main point here is that these reflections will be put to good use by your child throughout the process. Similarly, your child will later be given opportunities to draw on their responses to the interests and inspiration prompts in situations like interviews by local alumni, who will then write up a report for the admissions committee.

As you present this exercise to your child, don't do so as if you were administering a proctored exam. There are no right or wrong answers, of course, since what they are writing here are effectively notes to themselves. You might advise them to view the exercise as a journal or diary entry and to decide later how much of what they have written they ultimately wish to convey in a college application or to a college admissions officer. Encourage them to consider their answers to be a living document, augmenting our proposed headings as they see fit, and to leave plenty of space for additions or corrections, as well as thoughts that may come to them over time—including during a morning jog or even upon waking in the middle of the night. Defer to your child as to whether they wish to share their self-reflections with you, or with anyone else. The most important objective is that they be open and honest with themselves.

(E.) Behind the Admissions Office Door: A Brief Primer on the Holistic Admissions Process (And the Ultimate Audience for Your Child's Application)

At key moments throughout *The College Conversation*, we want to provide parents with some context on the philosophy and mechanics of the admissions process, and how admissions officers use information about your child (including information that your child provides) to help build a first-year class.

At its essence, the role of the admissions office and its officers is to help identify and assemble a group of students who will learn not only from the institution but also from one another. Their goal is to enroll a class of motivated students whom teachers can teach, who can support those professors in their research, and who can ultimately contribute to the social good of the university and the world at large.

As we explained in the introduction, most colleges and universities, regardless of their selectivity, engage in the holistic admissions process: a comprehensive review of the college application to gain insight into the whole person, as opposed to narrowing candidates down to a single test score or grade point average.

What makes up a whole person, at least as an admissions office defines the term?

That concept includes who they are as a student, the activities in which they engage (and the extent to which they show leadership), and how they approach their role as citizens of their school and broader community. It also takes into account their perspectives, which may have been influenced by their own upbringing; personal background; economic circumstances; and the environment in which they grew up, whether in the United States or elsewhere in the world.

Given these criteria, you can see the relevance and importance to an admissions office of your child's responses to the Five I's exercise, as ultimately translated and filtered through a college application. In the Application and Decision sections of the book, we'll go into more depth about how, specifically, a college or university admissions office evaluates and synthesizes the information provided in an application, as measured against that submitted by other applicants, and given the particular priorities of the institution at that moment.

There is wide variety, of course, in the relative selectivity of admissions processes, ranging from open enrollment, including at most community colleges, to single-digit acceptance rates at some of the nation's best-known institutions. The average acceptance rate at a four-year college or university in the United States has typically been about 66 percent, according to the National Association for College Admission Counseling.

The important point to bear in mind in the early stages of the college process is one of **alignment**—by which we mean alignment between a student's academic performance and the general profile of an admitted class at a particular university. So, how do you as a parent begin to help your child assess the selectivity of an institution in which they may be interested?

One way, of course, is to consult the various rankings of colleges and universities by the *U.S. News & World Report* or the Princeton Review. But take the horse race aspect of those ratings—such as the attempt to handicap one institution as ten rungs above or below another—with a heavy dose of caution. It's the raw data that underpins these ratings that can ultimately be most helpful and instructive.

For those who wish to research those figures and get a more

nuanced sense of an institution's selectivity, we recommend the **Common Data Set initiative**, "a collaborative effort among data providers in the higher education community and publishers" to provide a clear, universal pool of data pertaining to higher education. The Common Data Set provides information on the ranges or bands of the test scores and grade point averages of students admitted to a particular college or university. You could learn, for example, the SAT or ACT scores achieved by those students admitted to an institution who scored at or below the twenty-fifth percentile as well as the scores of those at or above the seventy-fifth percentile, at least for those who submitted such scores. Pay special attention to the scores of the middle 50 percent, as a barometer for your child of students whose scores were neither the highest nor the lowest. As noted in the introduction, most colleges and universities made such tests optional in the 2020–21 application cycle. Many extended those policies into the 2021–22 academic year. But even in a test-optional environment, these historical scores can signal the degree to which an institution has been competitive or selective in its admissions.

We'll have more to say about ways to use the Common Data Set in the section of *The College Conversation* related to building a prospective college list. But we wish to leave you with a few final pieces of advice related to learning about selectivity through the Common Data Set. On one hand, as your child begins to build a college list, they want to ensure that their test scores, to the extent they have taken any tests, don't place them at or below the twenty-fifth percentile at every college on their list. On the other hand, as we've seen, colleges and universities interpret test scores through complex lenses that may take into account factors other than the scores themselves. In other words, neither you nor your child should draw hard lines and conclusions based only on selectivity data, but simply be aware of it in considering your options.

PART II

Conversations About
the Search

(A.) A Framework for Your Child's College Search

By this stage in the College Conversation, you have encouraged your child to look inward and to reflect on the type of college environment (and the attributes of that environment) that might suit them best. They have dutifully logged those reflections on that initial index card and recorded their interests, ideas, and other I's that serve as an inventory of themselves as individuals.

So, armed with the results of that self-reflection, how can you and your child use those insights to comprehensively assess and analyze the DNA of particular colleges and universities? Before you can generate a list of schools you might consider, you need to first have a framework to evaluate individual institutions and then compare them to one another.

Here again, we'll use an exercise that Eric has found helpful when he speaks to parent and student audiences. We'll call these the Four C's.

ACTIVITY #3: The Four C's

Culture: What is the history and mission of the institution? How does that mission resonate with your child, as a potential applicant, today?

Curriculum: Beyond a mere listing of majors and programs that a school offers, or even whether certain courses are required, what is the design and aim of the courses your child might take over four years?

Community: Who are the people who make up the campus, what do they value, and what are the physical spaces that they occupy?

Conclusions: What are some of the outcomes (such as readiness for graduate school admission or career opportunities) that your child envisions at the end of their college experience?

For this activity, make a list of the Four C's, with their basic definitions. Here again, feel free to tailor those categories and definitions to your child's specific needs, and to then use this framing as a road map at every stage of their research. (One alert about those categories: there is a fifth C, cost, which we'll dive deeply into later in the book.)

These prompts can most usefully serve as a reminder of your child's preferences as they explore each college, whether on the most cursory visit online or a walking tour of a campus. They can also form the basis for questions to be asked by you or your child, such as in a group information session on campus or via the chat box on an admissions website. Consider leaving space for notes on admissions alignment on your Four C's list. That information will come in handy during our discussions about both the creation of a college list and the application itself.

Let's consider some additional context for and reflection on each of the C's. How, for example, can you get a sense of a campus's **culture?**

Every institution has a history, sometimes a history that is centuries old, and one of your child's assignments is to determine whether and how that original purpose is sustained through its mission today. At the University of Pennsylvania, for example, the current administration and faculty seek to honor the legacy of founder Benjamin Franklin by finding practical applications for knowledge. The "A" and "M" of Texas A&M University reflect the fact that its original name was the Agricultural and Mechanical College of Texas. Founded in the mid-1800s, it describes its mission today as a "research-intensive flagship university dedicated to sending Aggie leaders out into the world prepared to take on the challenges of tomorrow." Brandeis University in Massachusetts was founded at the end of the Second World War by the American Jewish community "at a time when Jews and other ethnic and racial minorities, and women, faced discrimination in higher education," according to its website.

There are also institutions grouped into specific categories, such as historically Black colleges and universities, or HBCUs, a federal designation applied to more than one hundred public and private institutions; Hispanic-serving institutions, or HSIs, each of which must have an annual student enrollment that is at least 25 percent Hispanic; and networks of religiously affiliated institutions, such as the Association of Jesuit Colleges and Universities and the National Association of Schools and Colleges of the United Methodist Church.

Other aspects of campus culture may be a bit more challenging to discern: overall campus spirit, degree of competitiveness and collaboration among students, general level of stress and anxiety, primary drivers of social life, options for religious observance and expression, and openness and acceptance of students with a range of opinions, backgrounds, and perspectives as well as ideas and identities.

Obtaining information beyond a college's marketing and messaging in these areas can take some digging. Jacques recommends using basic journalism tools to fill in some of these blanks. If your child is so inclined, they might seek out sources like student publications or contact leaders of campus organizations. Further along in their process, they might grab a notebook or the voice memo app on their cellphones and set about doing a few informal interviews of recent alumni and current students, including at the dining hall, on the quad, or even through expanded virtual options, including student-led tours and faculty panels. Informed by this fact-finding, as well as their self-reflection, your child may soon be able to determine not only how they might fit into a particular campus culture but ways they might advance it.

As your child thinks about **curriculum**, the question they might first ask goes to the very essence of a college education: What am I going to learn? Often that question leads to a natural follow-up: How is that learning going to lead to a career? On the latter point, we urge a bit of caution. Both of us are proud recipients of a **liberal arts and science education**, which has at its core a belief in the virtue of learning for learning's sake and in the power of being trained to ask questions, to think, to write, and to be an active citizen. We are also realists, and we are well aware that colleges have never been under more pressure to answer questions from parents and students about the return on investment of their education. The point we wish to make here is that no one can say for certain what skills will be needed for the jobs of the not too distant future, and students shouldn't take courses or enroll in programs solely because they believe they will land them their first job.

For this exercise you might encourage your child to envision their entire classroom experience in college as consisting of about thirty-five to forty courses. Those can be roughly split into three categories. The first is **general courses** (or **foundational courses**), which are deemed essential building blocks by the faculty and include such classes as writing, foreign language, and quantitative analysis. **Free electives** are courses your child will choose to expose them to subjects and ideas that were likely not offered in their high school and might range as widely as documentary film, archaeology, international relations, philosophy, computer coding for the non–computer scientist, and nutrition. Finally, there is the **major** or **concentration**. For an undergraduate, this is the opportunity to go deep into a field of study and interest, as well as broad, considering that an increasing number of majors cross departments and disciplines.

The best way for your child to explore the curricular options at an institution is online. Here we suggest they toggle away from the admissions website itself to the homepages of the various schools within a university, which might have names like the College of Arts and Sciences, the Division of Social Sciences, or the Honors College. They should then explore the various departments (art history, astrophysics, religion) within those entities. These departmental websites are designed for current students, which will enable your child to imagine how they might pursue a potential course of study. Some college sites offer worksheets that enable current students to lay out options for the courses they might take in the three basic categories we identified above. Online visits can be followed up with actual visits to classes, where possible. Typically, admissions websites will have lists of classes for which professors have granted permission in advance for prospective students to attend. In some cases a professor might even respond to a query made after a class visit or via email.

We referred earlier to the responsibility that admissions offices have to assemble a first-year class that will become a **community**, the third C. In many respects this process occurs in the physical spaces that are unique to that institution. Some of these are found outdoors, like the main thoroughfare that threads through campus, the iconic green at the center of it all, or the statue or clock tower that serves as a beacon, sometimes from miles away. For an urban campus, it could be proximity to a downtown business district; for a more rural college, the nearby woods, perhaps threaded with hiking trails, and for a suburban college town, the main street.

Indoors, college communities are forged in spaces designed for just that purpose: athletic arenas, museums and performing arts centers, as well as residence halls and lounges dedicated to affinity groups (LGBTQ, women's center, intercultural center) and thematic learning (sustainability, technology, language immersion). Some of these spaces may have immediate appeal for your child, while others may become more relevant as their experience proceeds.

The physical space where they will likely spend most of their time is on-campus residential housing, particularly during their first two years. For many institutions the college housing experience is a signature offering, not only of the community but the culture of the institution. Some colleges group dorms into clusters and have faculty in residence, programmatic offerings, and even dining halls.

Amid the rise of a range of social justice movements and other efforts intended to combat hate crimes, prospective students and families might also consider the degree to which a college's community is welcoming, and embracing of the values of diversity, equity, and inclusion.

By **conclusions**, our final C, we mean something broader than just endings or culminating experiences. Your child might consider their college years as a sequence of incremental steps and achievements that build on one another. For example, they might take note of the percentage of full-time first-year undergraduates who succeed in advancing to the second year at that institution. On average, nationally, that figure is 74 percent, according to the National Student Clearinghouse. Families should ask pointed questions about an institution whose first-to-second-year retention rate is markedly below the national average.

Another marker relevant to conclusions is an institution's completion rate—the percentage of students who succeed in graduating. Because an increasing number of undergraduates nationally are taking longer than four years to complete a bachelor's education, a key metric on which colleges are measured is the percentage of students who graduate within six years. Nationally, that percentage is just below 60 percent. Here, too, we advise that you and your child do your best to understand the factors that underpin an institution's graduation rate, particularly for schools with high dropout rates. A bit later, we will talk about the range of academic and social-emotional support services available at colleges and universities, which can make the difference in a student's earning a degree or other credential.

Retention and graduation figures for individual schools can typically be found on the websites of the schools themselves, using "Common Data Set" as a search term. For national statistics, go to the National Student Clearinghouse Research Center.

What are other ways to track the conclusions at a college or university? A quick scan of its website, perhaps on a page for career services, or a question posed at a group information session, might yield information on graduate school placement rates and popular first jobs after graduation. Many institutions will survey students at the end of their first year, as well as their senior years, and sometimes into their early years as alumni. The questions in such surveys often center on students' satisfaction and are sometimes even broadened to include parents to ask how they felt about their child's experience. If an institution posts results like these online, they may be found on the school's pages devoted to institutional research. They are well worth searching out.

Harvey Fields, associate dean for student success at Washington University in St. Louis, suggests that parents and students also explore the degree to which an institution provides support for students' career and graduate school ambitions. To what extent are the offerings of the career center integrated into the overall educational experience, including through local internships, possibly for pay or credit? And for students planning to attend graduate school, is there a preprofessional adviser who is making sure that they are taking the requisite courses in preparation and staying on track, and who will write their letter of recommendation on behalf of the institution?

Equipped with the Four C's, we hope that you and your child are well positioned to take a more critical look at colleges and universities that may soon be potential candidates for your child's college list. A lot will also depend on the potential fit for your child, and let's turn to that concept now.

B. A Word About Fit (And Please Note: It Won't Be Perfect)

If it hasn't happened already, you and your child are about to be inundated with references to "fit" in the college process—including the exhortation to find a dream college that is the perfect match.

You may have already figured out by now that the insights gleaned from your child's initial index card and Five I's exercise, when combined with the Four C's, can provide a pretty good indicator of potential fit. One note of caution: as the words "fit" and "match" are bandied about, we recommend that both you and your child steer clear of any expectation of finding an academic home that is perfect in every respect. Let's say, for example, that your child has narrowed down to six the number of attributes or qualities of a college or university at which they can see themselves. As a next step, they might rank those attributes: is proximity from home, for example, at the top of that list, or are size or setting more important?

Here, as an analogy, you may be able to share with your child the experience of buying or renting your first home or apartment. There were surely factors you ranked above others with the understanding and expectation that no home or community was going to meet every criterion, particularly at your price point. While your child should come to accept that no institution will be ideal, they shouldn't simply settle for the easiest choice. As they continue to get to know themselves and what matters most, they should hold out for a college with those attributes that they consider essential. All we are preaching is a managing of expectations.

One key component of fit, as noted above, is a college or university's location. For any parent whose child is contemplating attending a college that is a long bus, train, or plane ride away, the mere idea may be enough to put a lump in the throat. This is especially true for children who would be the first in their family to go away to college.

If you are a parent who did not go away to college yourself, the prospect of your child doing so could prompt a range of emotions: a fear of the unknown, and perhaps even for your child's safety (a feeling all parents share); a concern over a loss of control; and anxiety about the economic impact. The latter could be a result of additional transportation and housing costs that you anticipate, as well as, perhaps, a loss of the income that your child might be providing, either through their work for a family business or in a part-time job.

For some readers, there simply is no choice: for many of the reasons cited above, and others, too, your child must attend a college or university nearby. But for others, we want to make sure that you and your child consider keeping the door open to the possibility of at least including on your college list a few institutions that might be quite far away.

Chris White, the college counselor at High Tech High, has worked with a number of first-generation families over the years and counseled many of them about the distance hurdle. He advises such parents to be conscious of whether their own fears are standing in the way of potential opportunities for their children—including the prospect of attending private institutions that may have compelling financial aid packages, with line items for housing, meals, and even transportation, even if they are some distance away.

"And they never would have believed me, obviously, until we had proof in the end," Chris explained.

One mother who needed convincing was Monica Mendez, whom we met earlier, who sent two daughters across the country from San Diego to Gettysburg College in Pennsylvania. Her agreeing to do so took a fair amount of convincing from Chris, the children's college counselor. When Chris suggested Gettysburg as a potential option for her older daughter, Monique, Monica said she had a ready response: "How dare you try to send her over there!"

"That was scary for us because this is our baby going to faraway places that we've never even been to," she explained. But Monica was ultimately won over after Monique first visited the school (with a plane ticket provided by Gettysburg) and then the entire family traveled there as well. Indeed, Monique's younger sister, Julianna, was later admitted to Gettysburg and enrolled there in fall 2019.

When we asked Monica if she had advice she wanted us to convey to other parents with similar concerns, she said, "Let them do it. Because it opens up everything for them." She added, "This is a once-in-a-lifetime opportunity."

We can imagine, at this juncture in the College Conversation, that you or your child may be eager to start building a college list.

Before we turn you loose, though, we want to introduce a few supplemental resources that may be of help, as well as a discussion of the critically important factor of **cost**—the fifth C.

(c.) Adding Other Voices to the Conversation

Up to this point in the book we have framed the College Conversation as one primarily taking place between readers (and perhaps their spouses or another adult) and their children, as well as an internal dialogue between your children and themselves. At this stage, if you haven't done so already, your family might consider broadening those discussions to include others, and other resources.

The College Counseling Office at Your Child's High School

Whether your child attends a public school or private school, make it a point for you both to get to know the college counselor assigned to them and take advantage of every bit of knowledge, expertise, and experience that person has to offer. Some schools will post a detailed, year-by-year timeline of the college process on their counseling site. Whether you or the counselor arranges the initial meeting—and it could take place as soon as sophomore year—it is critically important that the expectations that you and your child have for the counselor are clear.

Be sure to put key dates on your calendar as soon as they are available. These could include a student-parent college night, which may feature a panel of admissions and financial aid experts; a college fair, where representatives from a number of institutions may visit and engage with your child in a process that is like speed networking, and where you may learn much as well; sessions led by visiting college admissions representatives during the school day; and a financial aid information night. Your school may also offer free proctored practice exams for the SAT and ACT, under conditions that simulate the actual test. Encouraging your child to participate in the equivalent of a full-run dress rehearsal, or full-length scrimmage, can be extremely helpful in preparing them for what to expect during the real event—and in identifying gaps in their readiness they might need to address beforehand. Your school counselor may also provide deadlines for registering for standardized tests and for the FAFSA, the Free Application for Federal Student Aid, as well as for submitting early and regular college applications.

College counselor caseloads vary widely, from a ratio of just a few dozen students per counselor at a well-resourced private school to caseloads that average well over a thousand in large public school districts. Please be mindful of the realities of what your counselor may be up against—and ways you can support each other to support your child.

Chris White, who is the sole college counselor at High Tech High, asked that we encourage parents to either take the initiative in reaching out to their child's counselor or to be responsive (and proactive) when that counselor reaches out to them, either individually or through a mass communication. "We just want to be here to inform you," he stressed. "And we need your support in this process."

Regardless of the number of families your counselor is advising, your school itself may offer online resources that can help guide you and your child through the key steps in the college application process. Among them are products with names like Naviance and Scoir, which are provided to parents at no charge. Using Scoir, applicants and their parents can manage college lists, track college visits, and ultimately follow an application from submission to decision through enrollment. Naviance provides similar features, including its signature offering of "scattergrams," which plot admission outcomes from members of previous graduating classes at the high school against factors like grade point averages and test scores.

To the extent that your school or district has subscriptions to these services, or others like them, your school counselor should be able to point you toward a tutorial and instructions on registering, including as a parent. We'll have more to say about your conversations with your child's college counselor in upcoming sections of the book, including those related to building a college list and making a final decision.

For first-generation parents in particular, the college counseling office can help connect you with yet another valuable resource: other first-generation parents whose children went away to college in prior years. Neyl Montesano, a parent at High Tech High who describes himself as a self-taught specialist in welding, automation, and other technical fields and whose own parents advised him not to go to college, sought to "plant a seed" with his own children by invoking the stories of successful first-generation college students. His son, Jack, acknowledged that his father's efforts contributed to his applying to the University of California, Berkeley, and he was not only accepted but received a Cal Grant, the largest source of California state-funded student financial aid.

Omar Monteagudo, the principal of the School for Advanced Studies in Miami, facilitates conversations between current and prior parents through one-on-one meetings and panel discussions. You might ask if your child's high school offers similar programming, and, if not, whether they would be open to doing so.

Resources That May Be Available in Your Community

We hope it doesn't sound trite or out of fashion to remind readers that local public libraries may have a trove of information related to the college process, including guidebooks and test-prep workbooks. It is also worth asking if there is a librarian who is familiar with these resources.

You may have even more success reaching out to one of the hundreds of **community-based organizations** (CBOs for short) in cities and towns around the nation that make available resources related to college access and affordability, particularly for students from low-income, first-generation, rural, and other backgrounds historically underrepresented on the nation's college and university campuses. Jacques left *The New York Times* in 2013 to join the senior management team of one of these organizations, Say Yes to Education, which supports young people from early childhood through college or other postsecondary completion in the cities of Buffalo and Syracuse in New York; Guilford County, in North Carolina; and Cleveland, Ohio. Other organizations doing similar work include A Better Chance, College Track, Harlem Children's Zone, Posse, Quest-Bridge, and Reality Changers. For a more complete listing—and to see whether your community has such an organization—consult the website of the National Association for College Admission Counseling, or NACAC, specifically the page titled "Directory of College Access and Success Programs."

Media and Other Resources

With the democratization of information about the college admissions process in recent years, there is a bounty of sites across the web and social media offering guidance, often at no charge. While we don't intend to single out or endorse any particular site, we do want to discuss a few online resources from what is an admittedly incomplete and selective list that may be worth a look. But we should note that we often have some firsthand knowledge of the people working in each of these organizations and their methodology.

- **College Factual (collegefactual.com)**
  Browse around this site a bit and you will find a series of decision tools, including one called College Matcher. Among its six components for fit are those labeled with the headers "Location," "Majors," "Social," "Academic," "Financial," and "Outcomes."

- **BigFuture (bigfuture.collegeboard.org)**
  Offered by the College Board, the purveyor of the SAT and the Advanced Placement program, this search engine provides information on qualities and characteristics of thousands of colleges and universities. With My College Snapshot, users can walk through a six-step college search: types of colleges (including two-year and four-year, private and public); location, including proximity to home; campus setting; cost; majors; and learning environment (including balance between studying and social life).

- **Common Application (commonapp.org)**
  While this is the site that makes it possible for students to apply to more than nine hundred colleges and universities, it is perhaps less well-known for its comprehensive planning tools and information on its partner colleges. Among its resources are guides and videos for how to begin thinking about the college process in middle school, how to prepare for college and how to pay for it, as well as a live chat function.

- **Colleges That Change Lives (ctcl.org)**
  Based on the guidebook of the same name, this site provides profiles of just under four dozen private colleges selected for

their focus on instilling a "lifelong love of learning" in their students. All are viewed through the lens of a student-centered experience and outcomes (or **conclusions**, our fourth C) once students have graduated. Among the resources listed on the site's events page are college fairs in more than a dozen big cities around the country.

- **How to Apply to College (coursera.org)**
  This is an on-demand online course, available free of charge, that Eric codesigned and coteaches in partnership with Dr. Sean Vereen, president of Steppingstone Scholars, a community-based organization. Among its objectives is to demystify the college admissions process.

Whether and How to Engage an Independent Education Counselor

Having considered all these resources, you may still feel that you and your child need additional individual support from an independent college counselor. This is likely someone unaffiliated with a public or private high school (although they may well have worked at a high school or in a college admissions office in the past) who has a consulting practice intended to provide guidance at every stage of the admissions process. The services they may provide, for a fee, include test prep, essay coaching, college list creation, interview techniques, and drawing up a long-term plan, including for college visits and the filing of applications.

One indication of an independent counselor's qualifications is whether they are a member in good standing of a professional organization like the National Association for College Admission Counseling, the Independent Educational Consultants Association, or the Higher Education Consultants Association. The IECA and HECA websites feature simple search tools that enable you to verify a counselor's membership, or to search for a counselor in your area.

As with anything related to college admissions, approach any potential engagement with a counselor with due diligence regarding any promises that might be made as well as the fees being charged. For example, no counselor, independent or school based, is in any position to guarantee your child admission to a particular institution or even to one of their three top choices. And make sure you and your child have an understanding up front with the counselor that while they may provide editing advice on drafts of a college essay, the original and final versions of that piece have to be the child's own.

We are in no position to advise you on how much you might pay an independent counselor, because so much depends on your budget and the relative value you place on the services being provided. But if you do wish to go down this path, we recommend that you talk to other parents, as well as students, about counselors they may have engaged and their experiences with them.

There are some basic ethical lines, related to maintaining the integrity and authenticity of your child's application process, that should not be breached by you, your child, or a counselor. Any temptation to cut corners on your child's behalf can have repercussions well beyond high school and college.

D. The Fifth C: Cost

Before embarking on the initial assembly of a college list, the subject of money—including how much you and your family can afford to pay for a college education—should be addressed. Financial considerations are every bit as important as an institution's culture, curriculum, and other attributes.

Paying for college was likely one of the points you listed on your index card early on as a source of anxiety. This may be the first time that you as a family have talked seriously about money, including your earnings and the savings that you have on hand to spend on college, as well as what you are willing to pay and your tolerance for borrowing. Also up for discussion is what you'll expect regarding your child's working part-time while in college or contributing their personal savings.

For those of you who will need some form of financial aid, take comfort in the fact that there are likely any number of resources you can draw on—whether from the federal government or your state, or from the institution itself and outside scholarships.

We'll begin this section with a few tips and prompts for initiating this conversation with your child. Have this talk as early as possible— even before they have started the college list, and well before they push the "submit" button on their application. Doing so can go a long way toward managing their expectations, as well as yours, of what is possible. Unless you have the capacity to write a check for as much as $80,000 a year (in the case of some private colleges and universities), "Don't worry, we'll make it work" may not be the soundest strategy.

This conversation may require some advanced preparation, including number crunching, by you and your spouse or other partner. "If you have a plan, I think it's easier to talk about the tougher stuff with your child," parenting expert Carol Sutton Lewis explained. "Even if you have multiple plans, I think if the child can see that you are serious about making this work, it's an easier conversation to have."

Given that this could be an emotional conversation, set aside an extended period of time when you're neither tired nor hungry or preoccupied with any number of other competing stresses. Also take into account your child's current anxieties and high school deadlines that may be looming. You might also give serious consideration to limiting this particular conversation to you, your spouse or partner, and your child, leaving out other children or other relatives who may be living in the home.

Open the conversation by helping your child understand that the cost of their higher education might be a shared responsibility, while emphasizing your belief in the value of that education. This is not meant to cause them guilt or anxiety, but to enlist them as a partner. It may be appropriate in this initial conversation to introduce the possibility of a family sacrifice over the next few years, whether it involves a vacation or a discretionary purchase, as well as the need for your child to get a summer job or plan to work part-time once in college.

"You don't want to burden them," Carol says. "But if they understand the degree to which the family has had to sacrifice and focus to pay for their education, this might give them additional motivation while they're in school, and maybe make them think twice about deciding to blow something off."

One objective for this particular conversation is to introduce the broad range in **sticker prices** for four-year colleges and universities, which is basically the annual cost of attendance (tuition, housing, meals, mandatory fees) that the colleges cite before any financial aid has been taken into account. These can range widely, from as little as $25,000 (at an in-state public college or university) to nearly $80,000 (at a private institution).

You and your child will have an opportunity during the construction of their college list to plug a few basic financial variables, such as your adjusted gross income, into the **net price calculator** that every college is required by the federal government to have on its website. By using this tool, you can get a general estimate of how much a particular college might actually cost you, though with the caveat that this is by no means a full financial review.

Before discussing potential options for financial aid, whether in the form of scholarships, grants, or loans, take a moment to rough out a sketch of your family's own annual income and expenses, as well as savings and investments.

We've cast cost as one factor against which colleges can be differentiated. The first step in roughly calculating the actual expense you'll face entails determining the availability of, and criteria for, what is known as **need-based financial aid**, which is awarded by an institution based on an assessment of a family's finances. Do bear in mind that no two institutions have the same definition of need, nor are those definitions necessarily hard and fast. Some schools' need-based financial aid packages are far more generous than others, and open to families at different income levels, based, in part, on the institution's financial capacity, including its endowment and fundraising.

Merit aid, which is offered irrespective of financial need, is based on such criteria as a student's classroom academic achievement, test scores, outside research experiences, and talents, including those that may be artistic or athletic. This is another important area where you and your child need to do your homework, whether through research online or in conversation with an admissions officer or your college counselor, to determine whether the institution makes available financial aid based on merit. (The eight colleges and universities of the Ivy League, for example, are among many that do not offer merit aid.) Don't be shy about asking any college of interest whether they offer merit aid, and if so, the criteria for those awards.

You can also determine, by research or by asking a college directly, whether it is **need-blind** in its admissions, meaning it does not take into account a family's ability to pay when making an admissions decision, or **need-aware**, in which the need for financial aid is a factor in at least some admissions decisions. The overwhelming majority of colleges are in the latter category, often because of limited resources. The reasons why an applicant chooses to check the box indicating a desire for financial aid are both personal and practical. But families should take such policies into account when assembling a college list.

To further prepare you for an initial talk about money and college, you might have a look at the website of Frank, a financial aid information platform we mentioned earlier. It has a number of free videos and other resources—under tabs labeled "Parents" and "How to Pay for College"—that can help acquaint you with the various expenses of higher education and ways to finance them. It has additional services that are available for a fee.

Charlie Javice, the founder and CEO of Frank, suggested to us that as parents guide their children through the search phase of the college process, they might bear in mind the subjects their children intend to study in college and possible majors (if they know at this early stage, which they may well not), as well as even careers they might be contemplating.

"That's going to drive a lot of the value that you're going to get from the institution," she says.

With this insight, Charlie adds, a parent could begin to imagine, however roughly, their child's potential first-year salary in a career of interest—which could, in turn, inform their tolerance for debt and their capacity to repay it on a monthly basis.

While we've shared at several points our perspective on college as a laboratory for your child to explore learning for learning's sake, Charlie emphasizes a decidedly pragmatic approach.

"The first question you need to ask," she says, "is what do you want to study? Because if you're studying something with good job outcomes, you have a lot more flexibility in terms of where you want to go because you could choose to stretch financially."

She adds, "The only thing you should care about is basically the affordability component. And it's a privilege not to care about it."

One last tip from Charlie: as your child begins to assemble their college wish list, it should include at least one in-state public college or university—which will typically offer lower tuition, as well as aid, to state residents.

For now, bring this initial conversation to a close. Assure your child that there will be options for them to attain an affordable higher education. But critical to that process will be the drafting of a college list that takes cost, among many other factors, into account, which is where we turn now.

(E.) Helping Your Child Build a College List

As you and your child have made your way through the exercises and activities we suggest above—and perhaps have had conversations with their college counselor and others—the names of more than a few colleges and universities may have been discussed.

It is finally time for your child to begin to put those names to paper—or, more likely, to tap them into a new Google Doc or an Excel spreadsheet. Among our objectives in this section is to help you as a parent to support your child in this endeavor and to provide you with a few conversation starters to ensure that your voice is heard. While some advisers counsel parents to take a backseat through much of this next stage of the college process, we believe it is a healthy time for collaboration, while being mindful of the guardrails and rules of the road that you and your child established earlier. Ideally the conversations you've had thus far during the process have forged a level of trust that can be leveraged here.

At this stage—and let's say, for argument's sake, you are reading this book sometime during your child's junior year of high school—you're probably working toward compiling a rough draft list of twelve to fifteen colleges and universities, based on the exercises you've completed. This preliminary selection doesn't mean you and your child are going to visit all those schools, or that your child is going to apply to that many. While there are no hard and fast rules about how many colleges to apply to—like so much in admissions, this decision will be extremely personal and tailored to your child— we recommend, as a guide, winnowing your rough draft list down to something in the ballpark of eight to ten schools. While you have surely heard about the outliers in your community—the children who applied to more than twenty schools—we want to caution you that preparing each application produces a great deal of mental and emotional fatigue. The average number of applications submitted by each applicant through the Common Application portal is five, a number that has remained largely consistent over time.

We've spoken earlier about the concept of **alignment**—including in the context of you and your child being aligned in your approach to the admissions process (**family alignment**) as well as you and your child having a realistic understanding of statistics, like the standardized test scores of the middle 50 percent of admitted students at a particular institution, which can be a gauge of their relative competitiveness (**admissions alignment**). Your aim in the next exercise will be to develop a list of schools that are aligned in both those ways.

To that end we recommend sorting the colleges on your child's list into three categories: **sweet spot**, **likely**, and **aspirational**. For this round, set aside sticker price as a factor, with the understanding that it will be among the issues that come into play as your child winnows the list further, or perhaps augments it.

Sweet spot—We all probably have our own definition of a sweet spot. If you play sports, the sweet spot of a baseball bat, golf club, or tennis racquet is the point on its surface that will yield the optimal hit or shot. For recording engineers it's that magical area between two stereo speakers where the listener hears the sound mix exactly as intended. In business it's the price point for a product that leaves seller and customer equally satisfied. For applicants, colleges in the sweet spot exhibit a harmony between admissions alignment (the chances that you think you're going to get in, based, among other things, on the test score bands we referenced earlier or overall acceptance rate) and the attributes you're seeking in a college. These schools are by no means a certainty for acceptance, and many college counselors refer to them as "targets."

While test scores are only one of many elements in the admissions process, your child's results should fall very roughly within the middle fiftieth percentile range of a recently admitted class at a college deemed in their sweet spot. If your child's college list has been narrowed down to eight to ten schools, consider having roughly five or six of them fall in the sweet spot.

Likely—Some refer to schools in this category as "safeties," which is a label we avoid only because it implies an assumption about admittance that simply may not be true, especially in the current admissions climate. That said, applicants should feel confident that colleges and universities they place in the likely bucket are indeed institutions to which they will probably be admitted. Again, while the admissions process involves a lot more than standardized test scores, we do recommend that for a college to be deemed by your child to be a likely, their standardized test scores—to the extent they took a test—should fall roughly within those achieved by the top quarter of a recently admitted class. A winnowed-down list of eight to ten colleges should contain about two or three likelies—with at least one of them a school where their standardized test scores would place them even higher than the seventy-fifth percentile, perhaps even close to the ninetieth percentile.

Aspirational—This is the part of the college list where we feel a personal and professional obligation to manage expectations. Some counselors refer to these schools as "reaches." In one respect, an aspirational choice may be self-selecting: your child knows that their grades and/or test scores might place them in the bottom quartile of its applicant pool, yet the qualities of that school align so closely with their own interests and ambitions that they wish to go for it. For some schools, being a reach is no reflection on the applicant—indeed, perhaps 80 percent or more of applicants to that institution would be deemed admissible by the admissions committee, and would do well on campus—but there is simply not enough space in the class. These schools may turn away upward of ninety-five of every one hundred applicants.

While we do wish to manage expectations, we certainly want to encourage those who are so inclined to aim high. We hope your child will end up applying to one to three schools that they consider aspirational—fully in alignment with what they are seeking from a college experience, but understandably difficult to get into.

A few final thoughts before embarking on our list-building activity:

First, we want to briefly elaborate on some of our comments above related to using test scores or grades as a rough barometer of admissions alignment. These are but two factors in an admission decision, but they happen to be quantifiable. (And for those parents whose children have not yet taken the SAT or ACT, the PSAT or the PreACT can provide benchmarks.) The qualitative parts—the person who your child is, the level of their community engagement, their life experience, what they value—all contribute to the decisions made by admissions officers and are also factors in whether a particular college is ultimately in your sweet spot or where you might be a likely admit. Which means that these decisions can be highly subjective, and therefore unpredictable.

Which in turn leads to a point about your tolerance for risk. As an analogy, you might share with your child that putting your hard-earned money in a savings account at the local bank may be less risky than spending it on lottery tickets or a neighbor's surefire investment scheme. In that spirit, we strongly caution against assembling a college list that is light on schools in the sweet spot, or likelies. Not only should your child include at least a few likelies in their portfolio, but they should be able to imagine themselves at those institutions and be excited by the prospect of attending any one of them. If none of their likelies clears that threshold, they should be replaced by others that do.

ACTIVITY #4: The College List

This is an activity for you and your child—and one that either or both of you may have already begun in partnership with your child's college counselor. For those already well on this path, feel free to adapt this exercise as you see fit. But for those parents of children who do not yet have a college list, we suggest that both you and your child set about roughing out a draft. You can do so together or separately, comparing notes afterward.

Prepare by retrieving your respective index cards. Your child should also have their I's and C's at the ready. As resources you can draw on the websites mentioned earlier as well as books like the *Fiske Guide to Colleges* and *Colleges That Change Lives*, among many others—along with research you've done with your college counselor and perhaps organizations in your community.

To get started, arrange a legal pad or spreadsheet into three sections—sweet spot, likely, and aspirational—and spend about thirty minutes brainstorming. A reminder that, at this early stage, you and they should be aiming to put together a list of twelve to fifteen schools, to be winnowed or augmented during the due diligence phase. Neither you nor your child should overthink any possible choice right now.

This stage is meant to establish a framework for the next phase of research.

As you and your child discuss your respective lists, you might review your original index card and ask each other questions that draw on the potential alignment and divergence of particular schools from the interests and school attributes you've discussed thus far. Some questions you might pose to your child could include:

* How does this school's community align with your interests and offer opportunities to widen your circle?

* Would this school's curriculum challenge you intellectually and push you to broaden your thinking?

* Are you inspired by the school's culture, including its founding mission and history, and do you consider those values to be relevant to you and resonant today?

* Does the prospect of attending any of these schools exacerbate or mitigate some of the anxieties that have surfaced early on in this process?

* Do you believe that each of the schools you selected is appropriately placed in the respective categories of sweet spot, likely, and aspirational, and based on which factors?

You'll surely have additional questions for each other beyond those suggested above. It may not even be possible to answer some of these questions at this point in your process. But they represent a strong start.

So where do you go from here?

If it works for your child, they (or you and they) could create a separate worksheet for each college on their rough draft list, using each of the C's (culture, curriculum, community, conclusions, and cost) as section headers, with plenty of space below for notes (theirs and yours) about each school. These notes could be drawn from your ongoing research, as well as further discussions with your college counselor and school visits. In the case of that fifth C, cost, we remind you that each college has a net price calculator somewhere on its website, where you or your child can anonymously plug in some rudimentary financial information and get a very preliminary sense of the potential expenses.

(F.) Conversations About Learning Style

There are obviously aspects of your child's identity and how they might mesh with a particular college that don't necessarily fall neatly into the categories we've laid out thus far. One of these is **learning style**. After watching your child advance from early childhood to high school, you'll likely have a strong sense of how they learn best, as well as the optimal conditions to ensure their success. Does reading come naturally to them, and at what pace, or do they need to be cajoled? How effective are their time management skills? Do they prefer to study alone or in groups? And in what setting do they learn best: smaller, interactive classrooms, or larger spaces?

Mark Allen Poisel, a former vice chancellor for student affairs at the University of Arkansas at Little Rock, thinks about that last question in a slightly different way: "Students can get lost in a large-school environment."

"On the other hand," he adds, they might not want to be on a campus so small that "everybody knows everything about them, and every one of their classes is with the same students."

The answers to these questions can fuel some of your research about particular colleges as well as the questions you ask on college visits. You might also encourage your child to imagine how a larger school can be broken down into smaller communities, learning as well as social, and how a smaller school might be able to feel larger because of the opportunity to take courses at neighboring institutions or to study abroad.

Also consider a related, more nuanced question: Is the curriculum for first-year students—which may include required courses—organized in a way that helps introduce your child to a new learning environment and lays the groundwork for ongoing success? These may include small reading and writing seminars, smaller sections for foreign language study, and courses that refresh and reinforce the principles of high school. For your child, such building blocks may be essential. Because not all colleges approach the first-year curriculum in this way, your child should conduct some due diligence at the front end.

Similarly, you and your child need to have a shared understanding of the academic and other support services that are offered on campus to ensure not only that they succeed, but at least initially, that they succeed in moving on from the first year to the second year. Many colleges have writing centers and free tutoring collectives in a range of subjects and also offer exam analysis, a diagnostic tool to review and analyze how a student did on a particular test and then provide strategies for improvement. Not all colleges and universities approach student support in the same way, and the depth and wide availability of such services can be a critical differentiator between institutions. Beyond student-faculty ratios, which the colleges dutifully publish, you or your child might also want to ask on your campus visit how accessible, in general, professors are to students, whether during office hours or in settings like residence halls.

Colleges likewise vary widely in their approaches to students with **learning differences**, and their particular philosophies may well thread through an institution's culture, curriculum, and community, as well as the prospects for successful conclusions. Marybeth Kravets, a college counselor and former president of the National Association for College Admission Counseling, and Imy F. Wax, a psychotherapist, have co-authored *The K&W Guide to Colleges for Students with Learning Differences*. The book, published by the Princeton Review, includes profiles of nearly 350 colleges and universities with descriptions of their various offerings in this area, as well as solid advice for navigating this process on behalf of a child with different learning needs. It strikes throughout a note of reassurance, as epitomized by this observation: "We know that students with different cognitive traits can do well in college and succeed at work and life, often at very high levels of accomplishment."

(G.) Some Thoughts on Standardized Testing

Just as you have long known under what conditions your child learns best, you have also observed them taking batteries of standardized tests from a young age. The SAT and the ACT, the two primary college admissions exams, are in some ways a culmination of a lifetime of being assessed, often in a systematic way. You might assume that no test they have taken previously is freighted with the high stakes of a college entrance exam, but how much do these standardized tests actually matter in the college admissions process? We hope you won't consider it a cop-out that our answer begins, "It depends," but that happens to be true.

There is, in fact, a wide range in the degree of weight given to standardized test scores, relative to other factors, across the university landscape. But in general, even at institutions that practice the holistic admissions process, test scores, when submitted, may be considered at the same level of import as the rigor of one's high school courses and the grades received in them. Which isn't to say that there are strict cutoff scores, at least not at most universities. But, as discussed earlier, there are certainly ranges.

We want to begin this section by offering a sense of which colleges and universities require standardized test scores. In general, many highly selective institutions had long required that an applicant submit the results from at least one administration of the SAT or ACT, as their own institutional research has shown that these standardized tests can be predictive of the student's success in the first year of college. However, a growing number of institutions—some of them among the most selective in the nation—have made the decision to no longer require the SAT or ACT, and you would do well to familiarize yourself with that roster. Those policies may variously be described as test optional (students may submit scores if they like but it is not mandatory) or test-blind/score-free (test scores are not considered as part of the admissions process). A list of those schools—and there were more than a thousand of them, even before most of us knew the word "coronavirus"—has been compiled by an organization called FairTest, or the National Center for Fair and Open Testing. Among the reasons why colleges or universities might go test optional is that standardized tests can be a barrier to otherwise promising students applying to that institution. Moreover, the schools' own institutional research may indicate other predictors, beyond standardized testing, of which students have the potential to be most successful on their campuses. Also, as was the case during the onset of the global pandemic in early 2020, some colleges and universities may temporarily suspend testing and other admission requirements in times of crisis.

Encourage your child to consider applying to at least one institution that is test optional. If they do well on standardized tests, they could place themselves more competitively within the applicant pool. Bear in mind that "test optional" schools still do report the range of scores submitted for the admitted class. If your child does not test well—again, relative to an institution's admitted student profile—they might exercise the option not to submit scores, which would place greater weight on their courses and grades. As you'll see if you look at the FairTest site, it is certainly possible for an applicant to put together a list of outstanding colleges or universities that are exclusively test optional, which for some students could serve to substantially reduce the stress of the college admissions process. (Note that test-optional schools may have additional application requirements, including the submission of a graded paper from a high school class.) Even if your child is strongly considering going the test-optional route, we encourage them to consider taking the ACT or the SAT at least once, if only to preserve their options.

The road to taking the ACT or SAT can begin as early as eighth grade. For the SAT, the preliminary exam is known as the PSAT; for the ACT, the precursor is the PreACT. If you are reading *The College Conversation* as early as your child's middle school years, you might ask which exam is part of their school's testing assessments. Neither of these exams is used by admissions officers when evaluating an application, and thus for most students they are considered practice tests or a source of diagnostic information. By "diagnostic" we mean that these preliminary standardized tests can identify areas of academic strength and weakness, which can then be addressed during the high school years with extra support and attention.

One scenario in which the PSAT in particular becomes a higher-stakes test is for those students who take it in the fall of junior year as part of the application for a National Merit Scholarship, a program administered by a privately funded nonprofit organization that can provide recipients with additional college financial assistance.

Some universities will even supplement the award packages of National Merit Scholarship recipients. More information, including on participating universities (known as college sponsors), can be found on the National Merit Scholarship website.

Be aware that by taking the PSAT or PreACT, your child will be asked whether they wish to have their contact information (as well as their scores and interests) shared with prospective colleges. Should they decide to put themselves on the colleges' radar screens, they may well be bombarded with promotional materials, both print and electronic, as we noted at the very outset of this book. Whether or not to opt in is a personal decision, but you might use it as a moment to have a conversation with your child about their feelings (and yours, too) regarding privacy. One benefit of opting in is that they may learn about colleges that they didn't know about.

Which standardized college entrance exam should your child take? If either the SAT or ACT is the benchmark exam in your particular state, then the decision has largely been made for you. Any college will likely accept either exam. But what if your child has a choice? How might they decide?

One important factor is your child's comfort with the approach and format of the two tests. Both exams are now more rooted in actual course content (the classes your child is taking in high school) than may have been the case when you took the tests—the SAT in particular—a generation or more ago. As a way to further gauge comfort levels, your child might even take free, simulated practice tests of both the SAT and ACT under timed conditions, whether administered online or in a school setting, provided they wish to invest the time involved. Of course the actual tests have fees and are offered only on selected days during the year, so both time and money may be factors in choosing whether to take one or both tests, and/or to repeat sitting for each. If money is a concern, it is possible to request a fee waiver through your child's college counseling office or in a direct request to the test administrator; often, a fee waiver granted by a testing agency will automatically qualify your child to have their college application fees waived as well.

If you or your child want to drill deeper into the approaches of both the ACT and SAT, as well as the scoring methodology, start on the SAT or ACT websites or order books from the test creators themselves that share actual exams from previous years. The website of the College Board, the administrator of the SAT, as well as the ACT website feature free test prep videos. In the case of the SAT, those videos are provided through a partnership with Khan Academy, a nonprofit organization dedicated to making available free high-quality online instruction. The counterpart on the ACT website is ACT Academy.

There are, of course, any number of tutors or companies that, for a fee, will help prepare your child for the SAT or ACT. Some do so in classroom settings, which can be less expensive, and others do so individually. The latter can be viewed as the equivalent of a personal trainer who can provide discipline as well as guidance and motivation. Factors to consider here are the potential expense, which can run to thousands of dollars, as well as your child's learning style.

Alternately, your child might choose to structure their own test prep academy, using the many fine resources available free of charge (including those referenced above). They could also form a peer study group and enlist a teacher or even a parent (if your relationship can support it) to play a role as well.

How many times should your child actually take standardized tests? One factor to consider is that the tests themselves, as well as the lead-up to them, take time from students' core studies and can lead to fatigue at a moment in their lives when they are already pulled in any number of directions. We don't recommend that any student take either test more than three times—in fact, research indicates that scores can level off or even decline with repeated sittings—and for some, taking the SAT or ACT just once may suffice.

Why might your child repeat taking the SAT or ACT? For some, the initial results may be substantially lower than their scores on a practice exam. Or perhaps after taking the test once, under actual conditions, they'll feel better prepared to have a second go at it—or have a clearer sense of the areas in which they need to focus before retaking the test.

Another reason to repeat the tests may be related to admissions alignment, if your child has their sights set on a particular school, or group of schools, but their scores the first time out are below the fiftieth percentile of a previously admitted class.

If taking the ACT, your child will have the option—for a fee—to sit for an additional section of the exam to demonstrate their preparation for college writing. This is known as the writing section. Your child should research whether the colleges of interest to them require or perhaps recommend this part of the test. If they wish to preserve their options, and again are willing to put in the time and expense, they might err on the side of sitting for this section. (In 2021, the College Board eliminated a similar, optional essay section of the SAT, effective immediately.)

Over that period of years that your child has been taking standardized tests, they may have been granted some testing accommodations, such as extended time, the use of a keyboard in place of a number 2 pencil, or audio or visual enhancements, as the result of a documented learning difference or physical challenge. Such accommodations may have already been set forth in an Individualized Education Program (IEP) or a 504 plan, named for Section 504 of the Rehabilitation Act of 1973. If so, it may be possible for your child to be approved for similar accommodations on the SAT or ACT. The applications to do so require documentation, including of the credentials of the professional who has certified your child's "learning disorder" or "physical/medical disabilities," in the language of the College Board's disability documentation guidelines.

We would be remiss if we didn't acknowledge that some children (and parents) have exploited testing accommodations to attempt to game the college admissions process. Journalists have singled out some affluent towns where as many as one in three children taking a college entrance exam have been certified as in need of accommodation. Such abuse surfaced recently as an element of the much wider Varsity Blues scandal of 2019, in which several dozen people (many of them affluent parents) faced federal bribery and conspiracy charges, among others, as part of what *The New York Times* described as a "brazen scheme" to gain admission to top colleges.

If you are weighing whether to support your child in seeking a testing accommodation, take a moment to ask yourself what larger lessons you might be teaching them. One of those lessons could be constructive—namely that self-advocacy, when one is faced with a genuine hurdle, can be essential to success, not only in an academic setting but in life. On the other hand, if you do attempt to cut corners, you may impart ethical lessons that could have far more resonance throughout your child's development than the score they receive.

(H.) Your Child's Background (And How It Might Factor into Their Search)

If you're a parent who has attended an admissions information session or reviewed a class profile on a college's website, you're familiar with the typical litany of statistics it offers: *Our college has students who hail from all fifty states, as well as the District of Columbia and Puerto Rico, and nearly every country in the United Nations General Assembly.* In addition to geographical diversity, the contours of that community might include diversity of gender and sexual identity, race, ethnicity, socioeconomic status, and whether students are the first in their family to attend a four-year college.

Although these data points may give the impression of a process that entails little more than the checking of a series of boxes, the selection of an entering class is far more human than it is mechanical. Behind each of those statistics is a seventeen- or eighteen-year-old with a unique, nuanced story to tell. Over the course of the nation's history, some of those voices have been historically underrepresented at colleges and universities.

Through a series of court cases dating to the 1970s, including those heard by the United States Supreme Court, college admissions offices have been permitted to consider an applicant's race, among many other factors, as they assemble a class, whether at the undergraduate or graduate level. As a result, colleges and universities have sought through their own search processes—namely their outreach efforts to prospective applicants—to make a priority of identifying and recruiting young people from minority backgrounds. This is known as **affirmative action**.

In an upcoming section devoted to how admissions officers take the measure of an applicant, we'll discuss how race and ethnicity may factor into their decisions. But for now we simply want to encourage all parents—and not just those of children from underrepresented backgrounds—to consider the degree to which a college of potential interest values diverse perspectives within its community.

If you are the parent of a child from an underrepresented minority background—or, for that matter, a child who identifies as

LGBTQ, or even a daughter who is interested in a particular field of study that has historically been dominated by men—you might urge your child to seek a deeper understanding of the extent to which students from that background feel isolated or included on campus.

What we're suggesting here is that your child reflect on how one of the Five I's—identity—might align with or connect to one of the C's—community—at a college or university they're considering. So, too, for students who may be the first in their families to seek to attend a four-year college or university—how welcome or supported are they on campus?—as well as for students whose family income may be in the lowest brackets nationally. On this latter point, one barometer is the number and percentage of students in a recently admitted class who qualify for the Federal Pell Grant, typically those whose annual family income is considered among the lowest in the nation.

In identifying and reaching out to potential applicants from underrepresented backgrounds, many colleges or universities may underwrite the cost of travel to campus, including a round-trip airline ticket, so that students can experience campus life firsthand. In researching these programs, often known as fly-ins, students can be proactive in requesting travel assistance.

If you're the parent of a child embarking on a college search from outside the United States, you might go back to our initial index card exercise so that you and your child can remind yourselves of the experiences and community that you're seeking. As with any student from a background that is not in the majority on campus, you'll want to know the degree to which the culture (another C) is welcoming. There's also the matter of curriculum (yet another C), and the extent to which it is inclusive and broadly reflective of the world as a whole. For example, is there a concentration of courses in foreign languages, non-Western thought and experience, and global studies, such as Latin America or the Middle East? One website that may be of assistance is EducationUSA, a resource provided by the U.S. Department of State. It has a tab labeled "Your 5 Steps to U.S. Study," which includes the critically important step of applying for a student visa.

A student from any background that is considered nonmajority, for lack of a better word, could take the same brief exercise we recommend for international students and make it their own. This includes asking questions about dedicated spaces on campus that serve and support students from a range of backgrounds. Some may be organized around an affinity or theme and may include kitchen and social spaces as well as housing.

If you have attended a four-year college or university, how might your child take your experience into account, especially if they are interested in attending your (or their grandparents') alma mater? These students are known as **legacies**. Later, we'll speak to the question of how one's legacy status can impact an admission decision, and how such policies are under fire in some quarters. But the point we wish to raise here is again related to search. One critical question is whether a family member's experience or history at a particular institution is reason enough to include it on a college list. Some students may wish to consider embracing that opportunity, while making it their own. Still others may wish to blaze an entirely new path. It's human nature that parents may have strong feelings—positive, as well as negative—regarding the colleges or universities they attended. While it may be easier said than done, we encourage you to separate your own emotions or those of a spouse or other partner (including nostalgia, and impressions that may or may not be out of date) in favor of allowing your child the space to come to their own conclusions.

If, based on their own priorities for their college search, your child expresses interest in your alma mater, seek out available resources for legacy applicants. These could include admissions information sessions during signature campus events like homecoming and class reunions. If, in the past, you have served as an alumni interviewer of local students applying to your alma mater, don't be surprised if once your child signals interest that the admissions office asks you to take a break from interviewing for that year.

(I.) Interests and Talents Developed Over Time

Whether it's figure skating, the oboe, journalism, painting, or independent science research, your child may have interests and talents that are the product of a deep-seated passion. If you ask them to identify who they are, they might reply that these are the very experiences that in many ways define them, and as such, may be the lens that brings focus as they seek to refine their college list.

This might mark a point in the college search in which your child can reach beyond an admissions office and contact a particular professor, coach, or program director. That individual can provide valuable details not only on their program or offering itself, but on the degree of commitment it entails and the level of accomplishment of the students who are currently involved. Your child may well be wondering if they have what it takes to participate in and contribute to these programs. That question is fair, and one that your child can put to someone at the institution who has helpful perspective and insight to offer.

In making such outreach, your child should be thoughtful and focused—choosing one person within a department or program, as opposed to a scattershot approach. They should also bear in mind that the people to whom they are reaching out have busy schedules and may not respond. Some admissions offices may have guidelines on how best to reach out to particular departments or programs, including through the contact information on their websites, as well as schedules of class visits and open houses.

Depending on the program, your child may be asked, even at this stage, to provide an art portfolio, writing sample, or a recording of a musical selection to help better inform such a conversation. There may also be formal opportunities to submit similar materials through the application process, which we will discuss later.

If you are the parent of an athlete, the process may be far more proscribed and governed by the rules of the National Collegiate Athletic Association (NCAA) or the athletic conference in which the school participates. This includes guidelines for what is considered permissible contact between coaches and potential recruits. A student who is contemplating competing in sports at the collegiate level should register on the NCAA website under the tab labeled "Student-Athletes." In addition, the web pages for a sport or team at a particular college or university may have a link to a questionnaire for potential recruits. Prompts may include self-reported academic information, including grades and test scores, as well as sports-specific statistics.

Some children who competed in a sport at the varsity level in high school may wish to continue their participation in college, though not with the same degree of commitment. Suggest to them that, as they work through their college list, they explore whether that sport is offered at the club or intramural level. One gauge of their commitment might be the degree to which that sport is mentioned on their initial index card, or later among the interests they identified. We also note that such interests may wane over time and become less of a priority not only during the search, but while attending college as well.

(J.) The College Visit

As your child moves toward the point of preparing—and eventually submitting—their college applications, there is a critically important bridge that lies between the search process and the application process, which they (and you) must cross. It is a test, both intellectual and experiential, to be applied to the colleges and universities that may remain on their list.

What we're referring to here are **college tours**—which may be virtual and offered through the college's website, or in person on campus. These offer opportunities for your child to imagine what it would be like to be a student there, and whether they can truly see themselves attending that institution.

"This is going to be your home for four years," said Matthew Boyd, a High Tech High graduate, who decided to apply to the University of Richmond in Virginia after traveling across the country to visit it and discovering the appeal of its open spaces. He found it to be "a big campus for such a small number of students," which met his objective of being able to "get to know my teachers, so if I ever needed them, they would know me personally." He was later admitted to Richmond and enrolled in the fall of 2019.

On a parallel path, you will be engaging in a similar exercise around whether you as a parent can envision them there. If our process thus far has been the equivalent of a series of snapshots, this is the point to pull back for a panoramic view. It's also a moment in the process when your child should draw upon all their senses to absorb that campus environment in every one of its nuances and textures.

While we believe there is no substitute for the experience of actually visiting a particular campus to experience all those intangibles, time, distance, money, and life events outside your control can be limiting factors. If that's the case, for each school on your child's list, check to see whether that institution has a virtual tour on its website or on the website of a company that offers these tours, such as You-Visit. These immersive multimedia experiences simulate what it is like to embark on an actual journey around a college campus and allow you to choose with the stroke of a key where you wish to "walk" and which buildings you wish to enter.

To seek out voices beyond that of a single tour guide, whether virtual or live, your child might explore a broader range of perspectives—including those offered online through resources like student and faculty blogs and student publications, whether offering traditional journalism or opinion. Via social media they can follow the admissions office on a range of platforms for official updates, as well as to learn more about programs and departments of interest. One caution: we don't, in general, advise you or your child sending friend or LinkedIn requests to individual admissions officers or professors.

While such efforts could yield a trove of valuable information, there is only so much one can experience through a screen. As perhaps the final stage in the college search, we recommend, if it is at all possible, that you and your child create a game plan or itinerary for college visits. Your child should also consider that by registering for a campus visit, they are demonstrating interest to that institution. Indeed, some colleges keep track of demonstrated interest, including your child's attending a college admissions officer's visit to their high school, which can be a factor in the admissions process (though hardly the deciding factor), as we will discuss further in the portion of this book devoted to admissions officers' decision-making.

In advance of a college visit, it may also be possible to sign up to visit classes from an approved list on the admissions office visit page, as well as information sessions that are specific to an area of academic interest or a particular school or program within the college or university. Walking around a campus fifteen minutes before classes begin, and fifteen minutes afterward, will provide an opportunity to observe its unique dynamics and vibrancy.

Where possible, your child might also reach out in advance to a graduate of their high school who is attending a college they plan on visiting and arrange a time to meet. In doing so they can learn about the experience of someone who came from a similar environment and the degree to which they felt prepared when they matriculated. While some children will have no shortage of high school alumni from whom to choose, others may have to seek out the few trailblazers who preceded them.

We have one other travel tip to pass along from Chloe Rodriguez, a High Tech High graduate studying at New York University who hadn't traveled much before embarking on her college tours. She suggests that you and your child draw up an itinerary covering not only all your college visits, but the activities within each day, "because kids, especially me, like to know what is going to happen next. 'What are we doing next?' You can just look at the schedule."

Depending on the extent to which money is a factor, you may have to be flexible about if or how often you accompany your child on college visits—especially in situations where your child may be able to book air travel to and from campus at the college's expense via one of the fly-in programs mentioned earlier. There is also the question of whether it is financially feasible to include other family members. Spouses or other partners might also consider a divide-and-conquer approach, splitting the travel itinerary.

In addition to taking expense into account, revisit the rules of the road you and your child established. You might ask them directly whether they wish you to tag along on these visits—and, if the answer is no, ask yourself whether you believe they have the maturity to set out on their own, or with a friend, and what expectations you have regarding their behavior. Of course, for some families there won't be a choice, given work schedules and other family responsibilities.

Some schools may have the capacity to offer overnight accommodations to your child, such as in the dorm room of a current student. This is a question certainly worth asking the admissions office. The admissions website will typically feature a list of discounted local hotels and motels nearby. It might also be worth checking the websites Airbnb and Vrbo, on which private homes and apartments can be rented. Likewise, consider whether there are relatives or family friends in the area who might be willing to put you up for a night.

Mindful that some prospective applicants may be traveling by air for the first time, Chloe said that in preparation for her college visits, she and her mother watched a series of YouTube videos on packing and travel tips. She added, "We just researched what you can take on your specific flight; that way you can learn what you can pack and what you can't." She also asked that we advise you to advise your children to "leave room in your suitcase," including for college swag they might want to bring back.

Quite often, students and families overlook visits to colleges and universities in their own vicinity, based on the belief that they have seen them frequently, perhaps because they routinely drive by the outskirts of campus. Even if that school is not on your child's list, it might still be worth a visit as something of a dry run, provided it has at least some similarities to schools that may actually be on their list. The purpose here is to gain insight and practice into how you can best experience a campus you are visiting.

ACTIVITY #5: Planning a College Road Trip

College visits are very much a long-range planning exercise. You and your child (and perhaps a spouse or other partner) should set aside time to gather at the kitchen table or in a home office where you have access to a computer and sufficient surface space to spread out some paperwork, including from prior activities, to draw up an itinerary. While you may be tempted to do this work on behalf of your child— or they may prefer to do it themselves—our general advice is that, at an appropriate point in the process, you find a way to do this activity together.

Depending on the point when you are entering the College Conversation, your child may be planning college visits as early as the sophomore year of high school or during a family vacation. While there are no firm rules here, we do encourage you to consider whether you are planning a college visit too early in your child's development, with the risk of perhaps scaring or overwhelming them. These are obviously personal decisions. In terms of timing, we believe you'll both get the most out of these visits if you've engaged in the activities we presented earlier in this book, while acknowledging that family schedules may make it possible to visit colleges at an earlier point.

In general, start thinking about planning to schedule college visits beginning the summer prior to junior year of high school and continuing, if feasible, during school vacations and national holidays, and on into the new calendar year and the summer before senior year. One word of advice: while national holidays can be among the times that colleges are most crowded with visiting parents and students, they might also be days when the colleges offer additional programming.

For this activity, you and your child will need:

- Their high school calendar

- Google or other calendars that include their schedules, and yours

- Access via computer to a navigation tool like MapQuest, Google Maps, or Waze, as well as airline websites (or aggregators like Kayak) and public transportation schedules

- A rough budget

While we acknowledge that ours is increasingly a digital society, we both see value in your printing and marking up calendars with highlighters and Sharpies, and perhaps even availing yourselves of an erasable whiteboard as part of this exercise.

In general, your aim should be to register for a college's group information session—typically led by an admissions officer, and perhaps current students—as well as a guided campus tour, which will be led by students. Some schools will offer information sessions and tours only on particular days, including weekends, and slots can fill up quickly. In addition, some schools recommend on-campus interviews, which also require prior registration. There may be restrictions on the point in a student's high school career when colleges permit them to interview (perhaps beginning in spring of the junior year). If it is possible to do an on-campus interview, even if it is not required, your child should consider it as an opportunity to ask questions of their own (regardless of whether the interviewer is an admissions officer or a current student) as well as to share firsthand their impressions and experiences of that school.

When scheduling campus visits, be conscious of blackout days—such as new student move-in days or graduation—when visitors cannot be accommodated. Also be aware of the point in the institution's academic calendar when you may be contemplating a visit. If it's midterms or final exam period, current student stress levels may be higher than normal. In an ideal world, your child should visit a campus when students are actually present, and not during a break.

As you and your child plan your trips, consider whether it is possible to cluster visits to a set of geographically close schools. We certainly don't advise visiting more than two schools in a day, given how time-consuming and intense those experiences can be. There is also something to be said, schedules and other factors permitting, for visiting just a single school on a particular day. Encourage your child to use part of that day to visit the surrounding area, to contemplate and take some reflective time to process the experience, or to spend an early evening walking through the campus more casually.

As you plot your schedule, be sure to build in breaks—whether for downtime, exercise, naps, or homework. For those readers who have never experienced a college tour from the vantage point of being a parent, be aware that they can be as intense for you as they are for your child. A lot of information is going to be conveyed in a very short period of time. There's also going to be a lot of walking, with some tours lasting upward of ninety minutes, so wear comfortable shoes.

Pace yourselves by not trying to plan all your college visits in a single sitting. You and your child may need breaks, as well as supplemental information, such as from an admissions office during working hours. At the end of this activity, you should have a draft master plan that might extend for a full year or more. But build in some flexibility, as college admissions offices may post their calendar of visit dates only a few months in advance. Also, your calendar and your child's may change.

Setting off on a college trip may be the most time you've spent alone with your child in a number of years. The potential of sharing a room together in a hotel may feel awkward. Be sensitive to all the emotions your child may be feeling, including fear or anxiety, and don't underestimate the value of a little strategically placed silence or time apart.

As you're packing for your trip, remember to take along the individual index cards, worksheets, or spreadsheets for each school, in which the five C's are listed—culture, curriculum, community, conclusions, and cost—with space below each for you and your child to record your observations, reflections, and impressions. In their applications, most colleges will include a question that essentially boils down to "Why our school?" The data you fill out after your visit will provide useful raw material for your child's reply to this question.

If you or your child have any concerns about mobility, and require special assistance, share that information with the admissions office before the visit. Pack an empty water bottle, too, as there should be filling stations at the admissions office or along the way. Bring along an umbrella and a rain jacket, though some admissions offices may provide both. During extreme weather, the campus tour may relocate indoors for a student panel.

If your child has an appointment for an interview, they might consider, as a general rule, dressing business casual. Ultimately, your child's comfort—not only in what they are wearing for an interview, but how they are feeling at that moment—is what is most important. For students who are not interviewing, the visit could be relatively anonymous, particularly at large- and medium-sized institutions, apart from signing in at the admissions office to indicate you've paid a visit. In this case, tip the balance toward comfort and allow your child to choose what to wear, though not to the point of sloppiness. In our own experiences on campus, each of us has seen prospective applicants who choose for whatever reason to wear the sweatshirt of another institution. If your child is inclined to do so, you might suggest otherwise.

You and your child might also devote some thought and research,

prior to arriving on campus, to where you might eat—a campus dining hall, a local diner, or maybe a renowned local food truck—not
just for the meal itself, but to be able to experience the overall environment. Don't forget to check on the proximity and ease of park-
ing, which should be posted on the admissions website. Plan ahead,
and build time into your itinerary for potential delays.

Have a conversation in advance about your child's comfort with
your asking questions at a group information session. Regardless of
who is doing the asking—you or your child—we suggest that you
prepare a series of questions in advance, whether you'll present them
at the session itself or in a one-on-one immediately after. Harvey
Fields of Washington University in St. Louis advises that you arrive
prepared with specific questions about student support services, including academics, social life, physical and mental health, and opportunities after graduation, and drill deep on each. For example,
you or your child should ask not just about the existence of a tutoring center, but whether it is situated as a priority within the campus
culture and organizational chart, with a high-level advocate, such as
a senior administrator. And to the extent those academic services are
delivered by other students, how are they trained and supervised?
Another possible line of questioning Dr. Fields suggests concerns
campus mental health services: Where are they located? To how
many visits is a student entitled? Who oversees those services? And
how long does it take to get an initial appointment?

You might also discuss with your child whether they wish to take
the campus tour together or to split up. Some colleges will require
parent and child to go on different tours, which can have the advantage of giving each separate perspectives to compare and contrast
later. That said, hearing and responding to the same information
together, and in real time, can be valuable.

As you and your child walk around campus, be mindful to observe your surroundings. Look at the flyers and other materials that have been tacked up on bulletin boards or that students may be handing out along the way. Pay attention to the information on LED TV displays, including messages regarding upcoming lectures and other campus events. You may also wish to check the events calendar on the college website prior to your visit and attend gatherings that are open to the general public.

Carol Sutton Lewis recalled that on each of her daughter's college visits, her daughter made a point of stopping three students at random to ask them a series of questions. You might think of this as the "current student" conversation. As Carol explains:

> She'd ask them what year they were, how they liked it, where else they thought about going, and why they decided to go to this place. For a relatively shy person at the time, she found students were very friendly while the responses ranged from the sort of brusque to, "Here, do you want to see my room?" It was a variety of responses that served two major purposes. It gave her a lot of information that she couldn't get from the information session and the tour, where you get one student giving your tour, one student's impression. It also made her hear how other people viewed it. And not everybody said, "I love it." They were honest about it. And where was I? I was sitting removed, somewhere on a bench. Because whatever they would say to her, it's going to be different than what they would say to me. I really looked at it as a valuable opportunity for her to see herself as a college student.

As you are leaving the campus, and before you get into your car, you and your child might take a moment to pause and look back. Do so with the intention of taking a few final mental snapshots—or just to draw a few deep breaths and to reflect on your experience. You might also remind yourself that simply by virtue of traveling to this campus and taking an extended look around it, you have reached a critical milestone in the search process.

Once in the car, or en route to the train station or airport, consider the virtue, yet again, of a bit of silence. Your child may be eager to hear your answer to the question, "What did you think?" and you may be equally curious about their own response. Be aware that your child may be looking closely for cues and clues from you that you may not wish to share at this time, with the impressions from your visit still so fresh.

Here again, Carol has some pointed advice for parents: keep your poker face, as best you can, and avoid trying to tip the scales with observations like, "Who wouldn't want to go here? *I* want to go here." At least at this early stage, refrain from comments like, "The cafeteria looked kind of grungy." To the extent you are pressed by your child to show your hand, Carol suggests you consider gently turning those questions back to your child to allow them to share their impressions. Back at the hotel or on the plane, separately or together, fill out your worksheets and then, at whatever point you both feel ready, compare notes.

There may be opportunities for your child to return to a given campus. Some high-school-sponsored events, such as Model United Nations or a debate competition, may take place at a college or university. Some schools also offer on-campus summer programs for high school students that may last from two to six weeks and feature classes taught by college faculty or graduate students in an area of academic interest. This can be a good opportunity for your child to experience independence, as well as dorm living, and to be around similarly engaged peers. Two caveats: such programs can be expensive, sometimes costing thousands of dollars. And while your child might learn much about an institution by spending part of a summer on its campus, they should know that participation in such a program should not be viewed as a strategy to gain a leg up in the college admissions process.

Before long, your child's college list will be set—and conversations about the application itself will be at hand.

PART III

---

*Conversations About
the Application*

(A.) Refining the List

While each family will join the College Conversation at a different point in their child's development, we're now approaching a critical moment in the process that is, in fact, governed by a fixed calendar, beginning the summer immediately preceding senior year. It is the process of assembling and submitting college applications.

In the coming pages, we will walk you through every component of the application, including **transcripts**, **essays**, **counselor and teacher recommendations**, records of your child's **extracurricular activities**, **test results**, **interviews**, and **financial aid**. When we refer to "the admissions calendar," we're talking about a period of time that begins on August 1, when the Common Application, among other application platforms, goes live (please don't worry—we're not suggesting your child file their application on or around this date) and that could run as late as February of senior year, which is the deadline to apply to some institutions.

First, though, you and your child may have some important work to do in refining their college list. We suggested earlier that the draft college list might have twelve to fifteen institutions on it. We then encouraged you to hit the road, whether virtually or up close, until the final list contained eight to ten schools—perhaps five or six in the sweet spot category, with one or two that are aspirational and a school or two to which they are more likely to be admitted.

Which may raise a question: How can you best guide your child to winnow their list, if it is still too long? With the search process largely in the rearview mirror—and we say largely because we know you may have some visits scheduled in the fall of senior year—this is probably a good time for you and your child to pull out the collective effort from the first five activities, including your notes from your college visits. Your child might then begin to put their college choices in some kind of order.

That order doesn't need to be especially strict, but perhaps you and your child can begin to put their choices into our three basic categories. Independently or together, you both can make an assessment of whether their list is light or heavy in a particular category. If, for example, your child has no schools that they would consider to be in the likely category, you both might have some work to do. On the other hand, if they have identified a dozen schools that they consider to be in the sweet spot, some pruning may be in order.

This could be a broader teaching moment, in which you could impart to your child that eliminating an option is, in fact, making a decision. And in arraying options alongside one another, they can clarify those qualities in an institution that they value relative to others. These may be difficult choices for them. For example, they may have to decide whether the availability and popularity of a club sport at one institution outweighs the strong sense of community at another institution. Or the seminars and more intimate learning environment at a small institution may be measured against the broader array of academic offerings at a larger institution. Please explain to your child that there are no perfect choices here, although some may have more appeal than others.

Some readers and their children will have the benefit of a strong college counseling team in their high school. We hope that the advice above will help inform you, as parents, for those conversations. Since they know your child well, we suggest you be open to your counselor's judgment. But we want to assure other readers who don't have the benefit of such one-on-one guidance, whether from a school counselor or an independent counselor, that this process is certainly doable on one's own.

ACTIVITY #6: Creating a College Application Requirement and Deadline Tracker

As your child embarks on the application process, it is important for them to know that they will be held to many deadlines during the fall of their senior year. While they can, of course, draw upon their previous experiences with deadlines in school and other settings, this is likely to be different. Unlike the soft deadline for a project that may have been established by a lenient high school teacher, your child should consider the deadlines that govern the college admissions process to be hard and fast. But they are also transparent and accessible, which means that a child who is organized (or coached by you to be organized) can stay ahead of the curve.

For this activity we suggest you consider using an Excel spreadsheet, Google Doc, or a piece of graph paper, depending on how you have completed prior exercises. Your child might even be able to expand or adapt the list they began in Activity #4 in the previous section of this book. Whatever format they use, down the left-hand side, your child could list each college that is a finalist on their list and then add a series of column titles arrayed across the top. Those could include application deadlines, including in the rolling, early, and regular rounds (more on these options later); fees; and requirements, such as for standardized tests and supplemental essays. They may also wish to include contact information for the admissions office. If at any stage your child created a login—such as when they registered for their college tour—they may wish to note the user name and password here, as they may be used in the application process as well.

As a model for this document—and also as a time-saver to track down in a central location some of the information to help populate it—we recommend downloading a PDF produced each year by the Common Application under the title "First Year Deadlines, Fees and Requirements." The grid contains information on the more than nine hundred colleges and universities using the Common Application. We have included a screen grab of a portion of the document below.

2020-21
First-Year Deadlines, Fees and Requirements

Updated 11/2/2020
*See bottom of document for notes

Courtesy of the Common Application.

For those schools that do not accept the Common Application, the relevant information should be easy to locate on the individual colleges' admissions websites. Your child may also have access to similar tools through their college counselor at their high school, or through online tools like Naviance and Scoir, should your school or district subscribe to them.

If your child uses a Google or other online calendar, they might consider putting some of these dates on it—with reminder alerts. Similarly, if your child is open to your keeping track of these deadlines with them, you might add the dates to your calendar as well, so that you can monitor that your child is remaining on task.

B. The College Application as a Reporting Mechanism, and a Moment for Your Child to Take Stock

On the one hand, the college application is quite literally a ticket to admission—a form with a very pragmatic and transactional purpose. Although application requirements will differ from school to school, it is not possible to get in without one.

But we want to encourage you and your child to also consider the college application in a loftier light. Every one of its elements— family background; what their teachers say about them; what they have to say about themselves; the choices they have made, academic and extracurricular—is a storytelling opportunity for the applicant, a chance for them to convey who they are and who they hope to become. When approached thoughtfully, the application also offers an opportunity for interplay among these elements, so that the whole transcends its component parts. Think of the application as a mosaic, a work of art in which small pieces of various materials are arrayed to form a grander pattern or picture. The emerging figure is your child.

The application does, in fact, need to be your child's—which means that we again encourage the establishment of ground rules and boundaries. Until now, subject to your child's buy-in, we've encouraged you to partner with them at key moments in the search. But as your child begins to create and assemble their application, you as a parent might consider ceding a bit more responsibility in key areas.

We are not advising that you abandon your role as a check and balance, particularly around ensuring that they are on track to meet deadlines. We also believe you should confirm that your child is checking their email for communications from colleges. Email, however passé it may be to your child, will be the preferred channel for alerts from colleges for notification of receipt of important materials. On this latter point, we heard a heartbreaking story from Matthew Boyd, a recent graduate of High Tech High, who missed an email during the application process from a college that was willing to pay for him and a companion—in this case his mother—to fly across the country to visit the campus. By the time Matthew saw the email, it was too late.

Just as they registered for college visits, your child will be asked to register for the Common Application, if they are applying to schools that accept it. Parents—as well as other adults, such as mentors or advisers at community-based organizations—can also obtain login credentials on the Common Application website to keep track of an applicant's progress in meetings deadlines. Your child needs to grant this permission, and even then, you can view their application on a read-only basis. This is yet another ground rule to discuss.

You and your child should proactively come to an agreement, early on, about those portions of the application for which they will have license and ownership, as well as for which they will be accountable. Make it clear that you are not going to write their college essays for them, nor is anyone else. In the same conversation, jointly come up with some parameters on the editing of those essays, and whether your child would like you to have a look and give feedback at some point (again, it's up to them), or whether they might prefer a counselor, teacher, or peer to do so. These conversations require planning and will yield dividends throughout your child's senior fall.

In addition, each college will have an **online portal**, accessible through a separate login. Ask your child periodically whether they have used these portals to confirm the receipt of required materials, such as test scores and transcripts. Please note that these updates are not all tracked through the Common Application.

(C.) Your Child Assembles the Parts: Opportunities to Render Their Experiences

The various components of the college application can be grouped, loosely, into two main categories. The first is academic and includes the high school transcript; standardized test scores; counselor and teacher recommendations; as well as, perhaps, supplemental recommendations, if they are provided by someone who knows your child in an academic setting. The second category is more of a personal inventory and has to do with your child's personal qualities and voice—some of those I's will likely come into play here—and will include their activities; portfolios, where applicable (such as for works of art or musical performances); interviews (on campus or with alumni); and essays.

We want to say a word about the readers who will be reviewing your child's application and making decisions based on it. You may have an image of an admissions committee as a collection of stodgy old pipe-smoking critics gathered in a drawing room to pass judgment over glasses of cognac. Or perhaps you imagine a conference room filled with accountants in ties and business suits, treating each application as a ledger and spreadsheet with points to be tallied precisely as if they were profits and losses. Or maybe you're even more cynical and picture an admissions committee clustered around a televised lottery event, where Ping-Pong balls with numbers (or maybe even a photo of your child's face) jostle to pass through a clear tube and be declared the winner.

In fact, admissions committees are made up of those whose ages may range across as many as five decades, beginning with recent graduates. Many went on to get masters and even doctoral degrees across a variety of fields, including education. Taken as a whole, admissions committees are also increasingly diverse, reflecting the demographics of the nation, not only ethnically and racially but also socioeconomically, including those who were first in their families to attend and graduate from college. On many campuses, faculty play an important role at the admissions table, particularly for those disciplines that may require specialized knowledge of a particular field.

If there is a common denominator in admissions offices, it is that they are populated by people committed to giving each applicant the chance to make their case for admission and to ensuring that each application is considered with care. Indeed, your child's application will likely be read closely by at least two admissions officers, and in some instances an entire committee. Which means that rather than tailoring their application to an imaginary audience of one, your child should picture a group of individuals with a broad outlook and perspective.

Earlier, we compared a college application to a mosaic. Now let's have a look at each element in it.

The Transcript

Given that your child is in all likelihood filling out their application in the summer before or fall of their senior year of high school, their transcript currently has three years of courses and grades—as well as their planned roster for the senior year. It may also contain information on other graduation requirements, like service learning or capstone projects. This is an official document that your child's school will transmit directly to the colleges or universities to which they apply, upon request from your child via the Common Application or platforms like Naviance and Scoir. In some cases your child may also be asked to unofficially self-report their courses and grades over the previous three years. Throughout the admissions process their transcript will be updated, such as when midyear grades from their senior year are posted.

The transcript is the most important part of your child's application—and it will be the first element considered in the evaluation process.

While you as a parent have probably been in the loop throughout their high school years, dutifully keeping track of their quarterly grades, we strongly recommend that you obtain a copy of their updated transcript and take a fresh look at it—viewing it actively and as if for the first time, as an admissions officer will. When that admissions officer does examine your child's transcript, they will do so alongside a second document, which is known as the **high school profile** or **school report.** This is a document that you can also request from your child's school (it may well be viewable online) that will place their transcript in a larger context. Among the pieces of information it will contain are an overview of the school's community (such as the number of students, demographics of the student body, and geographic setting); its curriculum (courses offered and level of rigor, including options for International Baccalaureate or Advanced Placement offerings, in addition to the high school's own honors classes); its grading system and scale (including, perhaps, the percentage that have a particular grade point average); a summary of standardized test scores (as compared to state and local averages); and the college matriculation choices of previous classes. An admissions officer will use the school profile or school report to evaluate your child's performance within the broader context of their particular high school. We noted earlier that admissions officers will evaluate the rigor of your child's curriculum, but they will do so within the boundaries of what's available to your child at their school, which the school profile or report will show. To the extent classes or activities at your child's high school were impacted during the pandemic, that information will be included on the school profile.

While the transcript, at this point, may contain only three years of data, consider that it charts ages fourteen to age seventeen and reflects all the changes and growth that your child experienced during that time. You as a parent may discern patterns or trends within this document that your child or their counselor may wish to reference somewhere in the application. If your child is a straight-A student, then no color commentary may be required. But there could be a larger story to tell with the support of this document. For example, your child may have shown steady or marked improvement in a particular subject as they progressed through high school. Or they may have suffered an academic setback for any number of reasons—not only because they were challenged in a particular course, but because of illness or other life circumstances. These experiences can inform the discussion between your child and their counselor, and between their counselor and you. There may be aspects of your child's transcript that could be addressed in the letters of recommendation from their teachers or counselor, in one of their essays, or in the section of the application where additional information can be provided—all of which we will discuss shortly.

Standardized Test Scores

For all the new test-optional policies at colleges and universities, your child may well be submitting such scores. Although this may seem like a straightforward reporting process, there are some decisions that your child will need to make regarding their test scores (including in conversation with you and their counselors) and some strategies that can be employed.

For this section of the application, your child may wish to have handy the college application requirement and deadline tracker that we suggested they prepare earlier in this chapter—with columns dedicated to whether standardized tests are required.

When your child took the ACT or SAT, they may have listed colleges or universities to which they wanted their scores officially sent. Your child can also request that these scores be sent officially at any time thereafter—though they should be conscious of application deadlines and the processing time required by the testing companies. A growing number of colleges and universities will also accept self-reported scores as listed on the college application itself. One reason they do so is that it can defray the cost of applying to college, as the testing companies charge a fee to those applicants who request that their scores be sent.

Whenever your child is self-reporting information, honesty and accuracy are critical. Do know that colleges will verify all self-reported scores prior to a student's enrolling. By using their logins for the SAT and ACT sites, your child will be able to review and print out their scores to date, as well as the names of any colleges or universities to which they have directed the scores to be sent.

For those colleges or universities that require standardized test scores, your child should familiarize themselves with those institutions' individualized policies on how those scores are used. For example, some colleges or universities may use the term **superscore**, which means that they will consider the highest score on each subsection of the test—such as math or evidence-based reading and writing on the SAT; or the four main sections of the ACT—regardless of the date on which those tests were taken. As of this writing, the ACT has also announced plans to allow students to retake individual sections of the test, without needing to sit for the entire exam, as long as they have taken the full test at least once previously. Whether they use superscores or not, most colleges and universities want your child to put their best foot forward. The colleges themselves will also use these higher scores as they calculate the ranges of test scores of admitted students for external reporting, including for guidebooks and rankings.

In the interest of accuracy and completeness, your child should self-report all of the scores they received during any test administration that they would like a college to consider. The colleges themselves will use the best scores. We're not suggesting that your child has to report every instance in which they have taken one of these tests. But if they received a score on a section on a particular day that they do wish to have the college consider, then they need to report all the results from that day. In rare instances, a college or university will require that all scores be submitted from every test they have taken, which the institutions will make clear under their testing requirements.

We mentioned earlier that applicants need to familiarize themselves with the standardized testing policies at each of the schools to which they are applying and to note that information on their tracker. But what about the many colleges and universities that do not require standardized test scores for at least some applicants? Should your child send these institutions their scores anyway?

The answer may lie in whether their scores fall within the range of scores from the top quartile of the previous years' classes. And as a reminder: even schools that don't require the SAT or ACT may still report to publications like *U.S. News* the scores of those admitted students who did submit them. Earlier, we suggested that if your child's SAT or ACT scores were below the bottom quartile, then they should consider that school to be more in line with their aspirational category. But in this scenario, the college or university may consider your child, based on their relatively high scores, to be in *its* aspirational category—meaning that your child may be a highly appealing candidate for admission, and perhaps even merit aid (a subject we will address later). In other words, if your child, perhaps in consultation with their counselor, believes that their scores could not only further the case for admission but also be helpful to the college or university's profile, then they might consider submitting their scores. And here again, that can be done by self-reporting (depending on school policy) as well as an official score report sent directly from the testing agency. Students using the Common Application can choose to self-report test scores to some institutions, while choosing not to do so for others.

As with so much concerning college admissions, there is no definitive answer to the question of whether to submit scores to a test-optional institution. In part IV of *The College Conversation*, we'll spend some time discussing the admission decision process and the factors that go into it. One factor that matters to colleges and universities is the background and life experience of the applicant. For example, a student who may be the first in their family to apply to college—and let's say, for the sake of argument, this is also a student whose annual family income is below $75,000 a year, but still above the median family income in the United States—would not be expected to score as high on the SAT or ACT, considering the correlation that researchers have demonstrated between score results and a family's income and education. In such an instance, a score closer to a college or university's twenty-fifth percentile might still be helpful to the applicant, and the admissions office.

If your child chooses for whatever reason not to report their scores to test-optional institutions, you might take solace in the thought that by establishing such a policy, those schools are sending a message about the relative value they place on test scores in assessing and predicting your child's ability to do well at their institutions. But in the absence of scores, the colleges may seek out supplemental sources of information—such as a graded paper, or a more involved essay requirement—to assure themselves and the faculty that, if enrolled, your child can not only do the work but also flourish.

Counselor and Teacher Recommendations or Evaluations

Most colleges and universities will require applicants to include a letter of recommendation or evaluation from their high school's college counselor, as well as two teachers. If that mosaic of your child's experiences that we asked you to imagine earlier was made of stained glass, then these letters are the equivalent of bright shafts of light streaming through a range of colors. They also provide texture and perspective. The recommendation section of your child's application provides them with three opportunities to demonstrate to an admissions committee how the educators who know them best view their academic work, as well as their participation and impact in a learning environment, to say nothing of the school community. These recommendation letters provide firsthand insight into how your child will engage with the university community and contribute to its vitality.

You may have already had a series of your own conversations with your child's counselor. The reflections about your child that you provided in those meetings—as well as, perhaps, in response to questionnaires—can help shape the contours of the letter that the counselor writes on your child's behalf. That being said, we feel obliged to erect a guardrail here. Just as your child's essays need to be their own, so too should you respect the counselor's responsibility to prepare an independent assessment of your child. In other words, please don't try to write it for them. You can rest assured that if you did seek to do so, the admissions officer reading that letter would likely see through the effort.

While recognizing that counselor caseloads vary dramatically— from a few dozen to as many as a thousand—we nonetheless hope your child has proactively sought to give their counselor opportunities to get to know them. Your child might consider writing a letter that would help a counselor with a long roster of advisees understand who they are and what is important to them. They could even draw upon their Five I's exercise. Most counselors will appreciate having that material in hand as they write your child's letter. Ultimately, the counselor's charge from an admissions committee is to provide as broad a perspective as possible on your child's life and experiences.

The letters requested by an admissions committee from two teachers provide an opportunity for your child to have a say in choosing those teachers. Considering that your child will be taking a range of courses in college, it is important that they choose teachers who can speak to their style of learning across different subjects. The way your child processes a great work of literature could be vastly different from the way they would approach hands-on learning in a science lab.

As your child considers which teachers to approach, they should not necessarily avoid those instructors in whose classes they struggled. For example, a student who is passionate about the study of history—to the point of seeking out their teacher after class to discuss material beyond the syllabus—might do well to ask that teacher for a recommendation. But let's say that same student struggled in a science course. That teacher could describe the student's perseverance when confronted with challenging material—earning a B that may have been hard-won—which gives an admissions committee insight into how a student manages to learn under pressure, such as they might encounter in college.

Your child should not choose two teachers within the same discipline and risk appearing one-dimensional. Speaking from the perspective of someone who has read tens of thousands of teacher endorsements, Eric tends to prefer references from teachers who taught a student in the junior year, as they can better assess your child's growth and maturity. But there may be times or circumstances when a teacher who had your child in the sophomore or even freshman year knows them best and can convey the most vivid rendering of them. In such circumstances, that teacher could be asked to write one of the two teacher recommendations—or perhaps to contribute a third, supplemental letter, if the college will accept it.

Your child may want to ask their teacher if it would be helpful to provide them any additional information that could put their performance in that teacher's class in a broader perspective. For example, the teacher may not be aware that that your child is holding down a part-time job or has a long commute to school—elements that could provide a deeper understanding of your child's life. Imagine a teacher who assigns a tremendous amount of reading. Your child could inform that teacher about how and where they do that reading, which could further make your child come alive to an admissions committee.

Colleges and universities have very specific guidelines regarding their willingness to review submissions of recommendations beyond those of the counselor and two teachers. Bear in mind that admissions officers only have so much bandwidth to review each application. The question your child needs to ask is whether an additional letter would be truly beneficial or merely a pile-on. Examples of where such a letter could be helpful include those from a coach or orchestra leader, your child's employer or a leader of a faith community. Each might provide observations of what your child is like outside of a classroom or even a school setting.

A word of caution, however, to those readers who might be tempted to encourage their child to seek out a letter of recommendation from someone writing under an impressive letterhead—such as a government official or celebrity—with the hope of impressing an admissions officer. Not only do such letters rarely provide much in the way of insight, but they also carry a risk of distraction. This advice also holds for recommendations from alumni of an institution to which your child is applying, and whom your child may know well. Each of these cases, though, is unique, and we want to refrain from giving blanket advice. In those instances in which alumni, particularly those who remain in active contact with their alma mater, are open to writing such a letter, both your child and that individual should temper their expectations of the impact it could have on a college's decision.

Activities

Whether it's the Common Application or a form specific to a particular institution, your child's college application will include a section where they will be asked to describe their extracurricular activities. The Common Application has drop-down menus in the activity section with headings like athletics, debate/speech, community service, cultural, music, academic, and religious, among others. There is also a drop-down labeled "work."

Before wading into this section, your child should give thought to how they want to knit together these various activities to convey to an admissions officer how they spend their time outside the classroom or, in some cases, how they extend their classroom time. This is also an opportunity for your child to explain how much time they have spent on their activities, and over a span of how many years, as well as whether those activities were interrupted due to factors outside their control.

Far more important than the volume of your child's experiences is their ability in this section to convey the quality of those experiences, as well as their level of engagement and the degree to which they have grown as a result. They should not feel pressure to pad this list, or to fill every available space in this section.

Speaking not only in her role leading the Common Application but also as a former dean of admissions at several colleges, Jenny Rickard explained:

Those little lines are not as powerful as parents might make them out to be. What is powerful is the authenticity, care, and thoughtfulness that students have put into the application process. Those are the things that really stand out. I would love for a student to look at their application and just be proud. And for parents: just reinforce that what your child has done is great.

To that end, your child should once again imagine the audience that will be reviewing this information—and think about how they want to present their experiences in ways that have meaning for the reader. So how do they do that?

ACTIVITY #7: Your Child Catalogs Their Activity List

The objective of this exercise is to have your child take an inventory of all their experiences and then shape that list so that it tells a story. As with any story, some details will be more compelling than others, and still others will end up on the cutting room floor. By this point, they probably have a preference for whether they wish to set up this document on paper or electronically.

Your child's inventory should mirror the format of the activity section of the application, so they should familiarize themselves with it in advance. On the Common Application, for example, the information requested includes years of commitment, hours per week, weeks per year, and whether the applicant wants to continue the activity in college. Then follow the categories listed above in the Common App activity drop-down menus, with space for the name of the activity, titles and leadership positions, and room for a description, which is capped at 150 characters.

For the purposes of this exercise, your child should err on the side of being comprehensive, in terms of the activities they include, as well as their descriptions of them. There will be time later to winnow the list that is actually entered into the form and to edit those descriptions. The goal here is not to create a formal résumé, but to instead begin to experiment with how to describe their experiences.

Once they've assembled a rough draft, they can then give thought to those experiences that are most significant and note them with an old-fashioned highlighter or the highlighter function in a spreadsheet. The criteria for what your child considers important will be particular and unique to them. For some, it may be the sheer time commitment that determines the rank order. For others, it is the meaning and impact that the activity has had on their lives, which may not necessarily correlate with time devoted to it. For still others, it could be the positions held (managing editor of the newspaper; president of the class) that they want an admissions officer to see first. By giving thought to those activities they wish to amplify, and in which order, your child has an opportunity to direct an admission's officer's eyes in ways that will make a strong first impression, as well as provide a cumulative experience. They should also pay close attention to how they characterize those activities, given that space is limited, and do their best to make these experiences come alive for the reader. For example, use active words—a softball captain might say they "led the squad to a conference championship"— and even tap into some of the emotional aspects of that involvement ("and while we lost in the state round, we felt proud of how hard we fought"). Again, this is less of a résumé than a narrative or story.

When they feel ready, they can use this draft as source material to enter information into the activity section of the application itself.

We want to add a word here about the relative merits of uploading a résumé into the application, which the Common Application, among other platforms, permits. Your child should bear in mind that a lot of thought has gone into designing a college application form that enables the reader—the admissions officer—to quickly find the information they are seeking. For this reason, there are two words that have been known to trigger a wave of dread in longtime admissions officers: "See attached." By drawing an admissions officer away from the application itself, the applicant risks distracting them or taking up too much of their precious time. All of which is to say that applicants should feel confident that whatever information they might be tempted to include in a résumé can probably be more efficiently and effectively transmitted within the confines of the activity section of the application itself.

Portfolios and Other Additional Information

While there is generally sufficient room within the college application to provide admissions officers with key information, your child may nonetheless feel it is limiting. They may feel the need for more space to upload a sample of their work (such as a science abstract, a musical composition, or a video of an actual performance). A section of the Common Application includes the header "Portfolio," which is where an applicant might transmit photographs they've taken; short stories or poetry they've written; art they've created; video or audio recordings of a musical performance; video clips; or digital media they've designed. No one should feel compelled to create a portfolio, as it is neither necessary nor appropriate for most applicants. Indeed, it is a portion of the application that is probably most relevant for students interested in specific majors and programs, whose faculty may be enlisted as part of the review process. But even in those cases, there is no guarantee that portfolio work will be considered in the final decision.

While on the subject of portfolio work: in recent years, as mentioned earlier, 135 colleges and universities—ranging from some flagship state institutions to small liberal arts colleges to the University of Pennsylvania—have begun accepting an application called the **Coalition application**. It is designed to enable applicants to build extensive digital portfolios, housed in cloud-based lockers, starting as early as the ninth grade.

The Common Application also includes a section titled "Additional Information." Applicants might use this section to elaborate on experiences or mitigating circumstances not necessarily referenced in other parts of the application, including in the college counselor's letter or by the student in their essays. For example, an applicant might use this section to explain how a concussion had resulted in an extended absence, or that their family had moved several times. Whatever the case might be, if there is a need to provide additional information or commentary, this is the space to do so.

Disciplinary Information

On their college application, your child and their high school may be asked for information about any past disciplinary action they received within the school or larger community. This is information that is part of their formal record, including misconduct (academic or behavioral) that was the subject of disciplinary action. The first step for you as a parent in response to these questions is to verify what information is on your child's official record. If the school is obligated, based on their policies, to report such an incident to a prospective college, then your child should also report it in the disciplinary information section of their application. Taking proactive ownership in this way, your child will also be able to provide background information and explain how they may have grown from that experience as well as what they might have learned from it. Depending on the college or university, they may also be asked if they have ever been found guilty or convicted of a misdemeanor or felony. There is a growing movement called Ban the Box, in which municipalities and states have sought to bar colleges and universities from asking these questions; more information can be found on the Ban the Box campaign website. Recently, the Common Application decided to no longer ask applicants about disciplinary history as part of its standard questions, although individual institutions may opt to do so.

D. Conversations About the Essays: Your Child Frames Their Story

We turn now to the essay section of the college application, which represents a critical opportunity for your child to combine the pieces of their mosaic into a coherent picture. It may well be the final portion of the application that they complete before its submission. Colleges and universities include essay questions on their applications for two main reasons. The first is to assess your child's basic writing ability, namely: Are they able to express themselves clearly and effectively, and how well do they organize their thinking? The other reason that colleges pose essay questions—including those that are supplemental to the Common Application, and specific to their schools—is that they are genuinely interested in the answer.

To provide you with a sense of the framing and tone of such questions, here are six essay prompts from the Common Application for the Class of 2026.

1. Some students have a background, identity, interest, or talent that is so meaningful they believe their application would be incomplete without it. If this sounds like you, then please share your story.

2. The lessons we take from obstacles we encounter can be fundamental to later success. Recount a time when you faced a challenge, setback, or failure. How did it affect you, and what did you learn from the experience?

3. Reflect on a time when you questioned or challenged a belief or idea. What prompted your thinking? What was the outcome?

4. Reflect on something that someone has done for you that has made you happy or thankful in a surprising way. How has this gratitude affected or motivated you?

5. Discuss an accomplishment, event, or realization that sparked a period of personal growth and a new understanding of yourself or others.

6. Describe a topic, idea, or concept you find so engaging that it makes you lose all track of time. Why does it captivate you? What or who do you turn to when you want to learn more?

The seventh and final prompt was more open-ended:

7. Share an essay on any topic of your choice. It can be one you've already written, one that responds to a different prompt, or one of your own design.

Regardless of which option your child chooses, the thread that runs through all these prompts is a desire by the admissions committee to encourage them to reflect on their lives and experiences and how those moments have shaped who they have become and who they aspire to be. This is perhaps the one section of the application where your child can speak most directly to the reader. It is also an opportunity for them to do so without a filter or intermediary— which is our not-so-subtle reminder to you to honor the guardrails and boundaries upon which you and your child agreed early on.

ACTIVITY #8: Your Child Looks into Their Rearview Mirror

In this exercise we want to help you as parents support your child as they reflect on their lives and past experiences—with the goal of their identifying the signal moments and details that will serve as the raw material for their college essays. These stories need not be epic. To the contrary, sometimes a moment that is on its surface inconsequential can be quite telling and revealing, especially for a reader who has little to no personal knowledge of the writer. This is a research activity—but the research is personal. What we're asking applicants to do, effectively, is to become investigative journalists by turning the metaphorical camera or recorder on themselves.

Let's pause to give some thought to the audience who will be on the receiving end of these stories. While it is possible that your child has interacted with a representative from the college or university who will be reading their essays—they might have met on a high school visit, or at a college interview—your child should not feel limited by imagining that they are addressing only that one person. In all likelihood at least two admissions officers will initially read their application, and it is entirely possible that portions of the essay will be read aloud to a larger committee or projected on a screen during deliberations.

Most admissions officers will save—and often savor—the essays as among the last pieces of an application that they review, as they will by then have some context for that reading. Others will just dive in cold. Your child should consider that either scenario is possible and err on the side of assuming their readers have no other knowledge about them.

Now, on to the activity.

Spread this exercise out over the course of several days. If your child is in tenth or eleventh grade, it is obviously not time sensitive, and whatever reflections it generates can be filed away to be retrieved when the application process is at hand. Doing this exercise early could also provide some insights into changes in mindset over time. But we've structured this activity for those students who are working toward the deadline of filing their college applications within a matter of months or weeks.

At the heart of this is a series of prompts designed to inspire reflections, almost as if your child were looking in a mirror. These reflections will offer glimpses and insights that can bring your child's story into focus not only for themselves, but also for those who will be reading about them.

Among the prompts that you might offer are:

- What is important to you, whether in school or out, and why?

- What are the experiences over the years that have shaped you, and how?

- Who are the people who have influenced you, and in what ways?

- Upon reflection, how have you changed as a person over time?

Each of these prompts requires a look backward, as well as inward. Your child may also find it helpful to project forward a bit:

- Armed with these reflections and insights, how might you shape or influence the college community you wish to join? And how might that community further shape or influence you?

One advantage to your child contemplating these questions now is that this exercise will prepare them for insights that the colleges will be seeking to glean. As you put these prompts to your child, feel free to recast or reframe them in ways that will be most likely to encourage their thought processes. It is also possible that some version of this exercise may take place at their high school, as guided by a counselor or an English teacher. For those applicants who don't have the benefit of that sort of professional guidance, you as their parent are eminently qualified to help your child lay the foundation for their college essays.

By encouraging your child to engage in this exercise over several days, you will help them be open to spontaneous moments when inspiration presents itself. All writers can tell you that ideas will bubble to the surface during everyday moments when you least expect them: on a run, in the shower, when waking up in the middle of night, or while lost in a favorite song. Suggest that your child keep a notebook close by for this purpose, or create a file on their phone, tablet, or laptop dedicated to it.

Once you've presented the prompts to them, come back together after several days with an invitation for them to share their thinking thus far. You might also tell them some stories that you remember about them that could jog their memories. Or you could even tell them some stories about yourself at a similar age, which could model for them what introspection is like. Remember, though: this is ultimately, of course, their story.

If the process works for them, they might engage in similar conversations using similar prompts with a peer or another adult in their life, such as a teacher or spiritual leader who knows them well. In the case of a peer, your child could reframe the conversation as a journalistic interview about themselves: What does that friend consider your child's defining attributes, and what are some examples that illustrate that point of view?

As your child embarks on this introspective journey, they should be on the lookout for anecdotes and resonant details that will make them vivid to readers. During his career as a journalist, Jacques was periodically tasked with writing obituaries—which, when done well, are less about mourning a person than celebrating their life, often the life of someone who readers have never met. If your child is game, suggest they read a few obituaries in your local newspaper. We don't mean celebrities but rather people who in the most unassuming way may have had an impact on the lives of others. What were the details and stories that the writer of the obituary marshaled to convey to the reader what was special or enduring about that person? This approach might be instructive.

Your child should consider this activity of self-discovery to be complete when they have collected roughly four to six examples drawn from their recollections, insights, or life experiences that might serve as the building blocks for their college essays.

After they've completed the exercise, we want to share some advice—from our perspectives as a professional writer and professional reader, respectively—that will enable you to help your child synthesize the material they've gathered so that it serves as the grist for a compelling narrative.

Jacques suggests the following:

1. A college essay is not a comprehensive memoir intended to capture every moment of your child's life in chronological order. Instead, it provides an opportunity for your child to curate their life story—and to **use a few vivid examples** to support a handful of important themes or assertions. Each story told—each memory recalled—should serve a larger purpose and be drawn upon to make a particular point, as opposed to merely filling the page. Ultimately, those anecdotes and reflections should reveal to the reader something vital about your child.

2. **The opening sentence or sentences are crucial,** as they serve as an invitation drawing the reader into the essay. In the course of a given day, an admissions officer might evaluate upward of fifty or more essays. Like the opening notes of a Broadway musical, your child's lead sentence will set the tone. But rather than being entertaining, your child should seek to be compelling—whether it's by opening with a thoughtful question or a relatable anecdote or an evocative image. The idea is to provide something of a hook.

3. Like a journalist, your child needs to **be conscious of word limits** as they outline and rough out their essays. For the main Common Application personal statement—in response to the seven essay options—your child will be limited to 650 words. That is roughly equivalent to fewer than two full pages of the book you're holding. For a writer, that is not a lot of space, which means your child needs to use it well—being careful to be focused, precise, and economical to convey the points they most want to make. There is simply no room in an essay of this length for tangents.

4. Your child should also **be careful not to be too brief or spare**. The Common Application essay also has a minimum length of 250 words. While we are not encouraging your child to pad their essay, they should nonetheless use the space allotted to fully develop their ideas.

5. Your child should bear in mind that **this is a personal narrative**, not a term or research paper. It will in all likelihood require multiple uses of the pronoun "I," which may feel awkward, especially to those who may be a bit shy. Then again, there is a difference between being self-reflective and self-aware and being self-centered. Your child's college essay should not be a brag sheet, but it should serve as a vehicle for them to convey pride in their accomplishments and growth. None of these lines is absolute, and they will know best how and where to establish the necessary boundaries.

6. Ultimately, **the essay your child writes needs to be a united whole**, with a narrative or thematic line extending from the beginning through the body to the end. While repetition should be avoided, your child might consider ending on a note that evokes or recalls the main thematic point or impression they sought to make at the outset.

We'll now shift from the vantage point of a writer to that of a reader. As an admissions officer for more than a quarter century, Eric has his own advice about what makes a good and effective college essay. Overall he wants parents to think about—and remind their children—that admissions officers are human beings who are spending upward of six months of each year evaluating, discussing, and deliberating. While they take great care in seeking to understand each individual, they have to deal with the reality of a heavy volume of applications and of their own limited amount of time to assess each submission. That said, Eric emphasizes that admissions officers place enormous value on these essays. Among his tips for your child:

1. **Direct the focus and attention** of the admissions officer reading the application to what is most important to you. Superfluous words or ideas are a distraction.

2. **Let us hear your voice.** An authentic seventeen- or eighteen-year-old voice (as opposed to that of a forty-five- or fifty-year-old trying to overly influence that voice) can be refreshing. It need not be polished or perfect. That the writer is a work in progress is what makes it most compelling.

3. Remember that **the main purpose of the essay is to get to know you**, because in all likelihood we don't. Give your reader an understanding, directly from you, about what motivates you, how you think, what you care about, and, as emphasized earlier, what matters most to you and why. By reflecting on these questions, you may well gain a better understanding of yourself in the process of sharing it with others, in the spirit of the Discovery section of this book.

4. **Avoid the temptation to be too formulaic or linear.** Or, to put it another way, avoid drafting an essay that, in effect, reads as if A + B + C + D equals the logical conclusion that you are the perfect candidate for the college in question. Eric has read more than his share of these, and they are often as predictable as they are contrived.

5. **Be willing to embrace complexity and nuance** and accept that the various parts of your life or the range of your priorities or the experiences that you have had may not necessarily lend themselves to an easy summary. Some of the most compelling essays that Eric has read were crafted

by students genuinely wrestling with seeming dichotomies: the precision of an engineer and the spontaneity of an artist; the poet and the scientist; the fiscal conservative who prizes social justice. The point here is that human beings are multidimensional, and your college essay should try to capture that.

6. **Sometimes one story or experience can stand alone** in supporting your college essay, if explored with depth and sufficient reflection. For example, Eric recalls an essay by a young woman who described driving a beat-up Volkswagen to visit her grandmother as a metaphor for her own youth and childhood, told through such details as the stickers affixed to the bumper, the music on the radio, and the feel of the air with the windows down. That Eric first read this essay more than two decades ago should say something about the endurance and staying power of the imagery—and the effectiveness of the author's using it to convey who she was.

7. **Take with a grain of salt those so-called hard and fast rules** proclaiming that a particular college admissions essay topic works, or does not. For example, more than a few advice books will tell you to avoid an essay about a grandparent or the road less traveled. The example just cited by Eric included both of these themes—while still being insightful and therefore compelling. The lesson here is that the theme may be less important than what you actually have to say about it, from your unique experience or perspective.

Much of Eric's advice is especially relevant to those seven essay prompts offered as options in the Common Application. But as mentioned earlier, many colleges will also include supplemental essay questions. At their essence these questions are often intended to gauge students' knowledge about the schools to which they are applying, and why they believe those colleges would be a suitable fit. But admissions offices may also use their supplemental essay questions to convey important information to applicants about what they as institutions value in their student bodies, classrooms, and broader communities.

As an example, the undergraduate application to the University of Pennsylvania for the Class of 2024 included the following two supplemental essay questions. By considering the thinking behind them, parents and students may be able to analyze other institutions' supplemental essay questions with a more critical eye.

- How did you discover your intellectual and academic interests, and how will you explore them at the University of Pennsylvania? Please respond considering the specific undergraduate school you have selected. (300–450 words)

- At Penn, learning and growth happen outside of the classroom, too. How will you explore the community at Penn? Consider how this community will help shape your perspective and identity, and how your identity and perspective will help shape this community. (150–200 words)

In the case of the first question, Eric and his admissions colleagues (along with faculty and administrators who were asked to weigh in) sought applicants' firsthand testimony about themselves as thinkers ("intellectual") and students ("academic"). The second part of the question is intended to yield responses that will be of value not only to the admissions office, but also to the faculty and advisers who work directly with students in the university's undergraduate schools and specialized programs. Quite simply, the latter audience wants to know the interests and motivations of the students whom they might be teaching and supporting over the next four years.

The main objective of the second question is to ascertain how a student, if admitted and enrolled, would have an impact on the university community, as well as how that community might have an impact on the student. In posing the question in this way, the university is conveying to the applicant that it believes each and every voice matters, and that the opportunity exists for all students to learn from one another.

This is the moment when the exercises we put your child through regarding the I's and C's converge. For example, your child's sense of how their identity and interests would find a home in a specific campus community and its culture can fuel their responses to supplemental questions like these, regardless of precisely how the university frames them.

At this point in the process, your child should, at the very least, have in hand some roughly drafted responses to the Common Application prompts, or similar questions in other applications, as well as to the supplemental essay questions from the institutions to which they will be applying. This might be an appropriate time for them to get some feedback, whether from their counselor, a teacher, a peer, or perhaps you, if that is something that feels comfortable to you both under the ground rules you established early on.

"You have to show somebody," Carol Sutton Lewis told her own child. Speaking to us, she stressed the need for involving "a friend, somebody who likes to write, somebody who can ensure there are no errors. There has to be some other person's eyes on this other than your child's."

Matthew Boyd, a student from High Tech High whom we introduced earlier, emphasized the value of enlisting teachers as proofreaders. "Always ask teachers for help, ask people you believe are writing geniuses for help," he said. "I asked *all* the English teachers."

As your child solicits feedback on their essay drafts, they might ask you questions like these, feeling free to reframe them in their own voice:

- Does this essay convey the essential elements of who I am as a student and a person, as well as an individual and a community member?

- Are the examples offered in support of these elements vivid and compelling?

- Even in its roughest form, is the writing clear and well organized, and does it flow?

- Are there ideas I might add or explore with more depth? Are there passages I might cut?

They should also be mindful of the deadlines at the schools to which they are applying and, particularly in the case of the supplemental essays, allow sufficient time and space to research, write, revise, and complete them. They might wish to include in their application tracker some self-imposed deadlines for when they want to complete the various supplements—which, if they are not careful, can stack up like flights trying to land in the fog at a busy airport.

As a final gut check before your child puts the final touches to their essays, you might suggest that they consider reading them aloud, including privately to themselves. Good writers often find that by doing so, they can catch a grammatical error, an omitted word, or an awkward phrase.

(E.) Application Plans

Now that we have provided a primer on the various components of an application, we want to walk you as parents though the various college application plans—including early and regular applications, and the various rules that govern them. In this section, we will provide you with some definitions. We will then discuss the strategies that your child and you might use to determine which application plan is best, given their interests, objectives, and other factors.

Rolling Admission

Institutions that use **rolling admission** plans will consider students' applications on a first-come, first-serve basis, typically beginning around September 1 and continuing until the first-year class is full, which could be as late as the following spring. The colleges and universities that use such plans are often state universities, including Arizona State, Michigan State, Penn State, and the University of Alabama. Schools with rolling admission plans will often make an admission decision on a given applicant in two months or less. Some, such as Penn State, may divide their rolling admission calendar into tiers, with a priority submission deadline in late November, for example, that assures a decision by the end of January.

One advantage to institutions that use such plans is that it helps manage the flow of submissions and the processing of application materials. An advantage for applicants is the opportunity to know, early in the calendar, that they have already secured an appealing option for where they might go to college, with no obligation by the student to attend. And that knowledge can help shape the remainder of your child's list, and perhaps even prompt them to eliminate other potential schools.

Early Action (Including Single Choice and Restrictive)

In general, colleges that offer students the option of submitting an **early action** application are providing them an opportunity to get a nonbinding decision around mid-December. **Nonbinding** means that the student is under no obligation to attend if admitted. While this may sound like a priority rolling admission process, one critical difference is that colleges with early action plans typically review all those applicants as a pool, in the context of all those students who met the early action deadline, usually on or around November 1. Unless otherwise indicated a student can apply to as many early action plans as they like. The notable exception are those colleges or universities that label their early action plans **restrictive** or **single choice**. Students who apply under such programs attest to that institution that the only other early applications that they may submit will be to a public college or university with a nonbinding application plan and, in some cases, to international institutions with such plans.

Early Decision

Early decision programs typically have a November 1 deadline with a decision communicated by the university by mid-December. The critical difference in this plan is that a student must commit in advance to attend that institution if accepted, and to withdraw all other applications. Colleges take that advance commitment seriously. Before your child can submit their application, they—as well as you and their school counselor—will all be asked to sign an early decision agreement. On the Common Application Early Decision Agreement form, for example, the following two statements appear in bold: **"Early Decision (ED) is the application process in which students make a commitment to a first-choice institution where, if admitted, they definitely will enroll."** All three signatories on the form also acknowledge: **"If you are accepted under an Early Decision plan, you must promptly withdraw the applications submitted to other colleges and universities and make no additional applications to any other university in any country."**

Early Decision II

Institutions that offer students the opportunity to apply under an **early decision II** (or EDII) plan generally follow the binding rules for early decision set forth above, but with a slightly modified calendar. Deadlines for applying are typically in early to mid-January, with a decision rendered in late February. Colleges that employ such plans do so, in part, to give your child more time to consider their college list—at a point in time when they might have already received other decisions under other plans.

Regular Decision

The majority of applicants to the nation's colleges and universities will apply under **regular decision** plans. Application deadlines at these schools may range from January 1 to as far out as February 15. Students who submit a regular application and are accepted are under no obligation to attend and will be able to weigh their options when they've heard from all their schools. Most institutions will try to communicate a regular admission decision to an applicant by late March or early April in order to give the student time to make a final decision by May 1, which has long been known as the National Candidates Reply Date. In the fall of 2019 the National Association for College Admission Counseling, a membership group of more than fifteen thousand college admissions professionals, made a decision in response to an antitrust investigation by the U.S. Department of Justice that has relevance here. It struck from its code of ethics several mandatory provisions that restricted the ability of colleges and universities to recruit prospective students, including after May 1, a prohibition that the association believed to be in the interest of students but that the Justice Department considered anti-competitive. Later, the association's leadership recommended to its membership that it approve a revised code that would strike all other mandatory provisions—including a reference to May 1 as a universal deadline for student decisions, which would instead leave it to individual institutions to set that date. Your child should therefore be aware of the deadlines for submitting a deposit, for the purpose of holding a place, at every institution to which they are admitted, as those dates may now vary. By missing such a date, your child may jeopardize their spot in the incoming class.

Transfer

Our focus in this part of the book has been on application plans for students applying directly from high school. In part V, where we discuss the transition throughout the first year of college, we'll spend some time discussing the Transfer Conversation, for those students who may be contemplating a change. Suffice it to say here that while many of the components of the transfer application process are similar—transcripts, recommendations, and essays are all required—the rules and deadlines are far less standardized.

(F.) Assessing Whether an Early Application Plan May Be Best for Your Child

Now that we have provided you as parents with a basic glossary of admissions plans, we want to turn to the question of whether your child might consider submitting an early application—which we'll define as any plan that has a deadline prior to January 1. We'll also equip you with some questions to ask your child to help inform which of those plans might be most suitable.

As we move into the strategic portion of the application process, you and your child will want to have close at hand any of the exercises you have completed up to this point, as those reflections will help you both come to some decisions. For example, if your child is contemplating making a binding commitment to an institution up front, there should be strong alignment between their initial index card (characteristics of the college environment they are seeking), along with their I's (including their reflections on their identity) and C's (that institution's culture and community).

For those readers whose children have the benefit of access to college counseling—whether through their high school or a community-based organization, or possibly a certified independent counselor—this juncture in the process is so critical that you should be sure to draw upon all the guidance available.

Just as your child needs to engage in some self-reflection prior to submitting an early application, they must also ensure that they keep a close eye on the logistics. This is a good point for them to consult their application requirement and deadline tracker. They can't apply early, for example, if they haven't taken the necessary standardized tests for those schools that require them. (One caveat: some schools with early application plans that have November 1 deadlines may consider the results of tests taken later that month; your child should consult the guidelines provided by that school and also decide, from an emotional perspective, whether they are able to manage the additional pressure.)

Assuming that your child has met the requirements to submit an early application, let's turn to the question of how you might help guide them through the process of determining whether applying early makes sense.

ACTIVITY #9: A Preflight Checklist for Those Considering Flying Early

Imagine for the purpose of this exercise that your child is an airline pilot, deciding whether they are ready to depart from the gate a bit early and, if so, which route to take. You are the copilot, walking them through a series of final safety checks and supporting them as they determine the best flight path.

If your child is considering applying under an early plan—whether binding or nonbinding—some of the relevant questions you might ask them are:

* As you reflect on some of the concerns about the process that you may have flagged during earlier activities in this book—such as an institution's distance from home or its size—**are the institution's basic qualities consistent with some of your earlier assumptions and preferences**? And if so, are those assumptions and preferences still relevant?

* **Where does the institution under consideration fit** within the categories on your college list—likely, sweet spot, and aspirational—**and to what extent are you comfortable with the relative risk** of the outcome? If the school is in the likely

category and particularly if the decision is binding, are they going to be satisfied? Similarly, if the school is in the aspirational category, are you prepared for potential disappointment?

- Do the results of your grades and standardized test scores thus far suggest you would be a competitive applicant early—or **would you benefit from the time to show more grades** through the senior year, as well as any additional retesting?

- **Did you give your teachers sufficient lead time** to meet the deadlines of submitting recommendations under an early application plan? And are you **satisfied that your essays are ready** to be submitted?

- **Is financial aid a factor?** Particularly if you are admitted under a binding early decision plan, are we as a family comfortable with not being able to compare financial aid packages from other institutions?

- And finally, if you are admitted under a binding applicant plan, are you **prepared emotionally to pass up the potential opportunity** for admission to all the other colleges and universities on your list and embrace this one choice?

Now, like a good copilot, you'll need to support your child's analysis of their responses to these questions and help them come to a conclusion. This is particularly the case for those considering whether binding early decision constitutes their best flight plan—or whether they might better point themselves toward another course.

If you and your child haven't already had this conversation, this may be one of the final opportunities to do so.

One consideration to which we want to return is financial aid. Many colleges with binding early decision plans will work with your family to try to make that education affordable. But your interpretation of what you can afford may differ from the college's calculation of your **expected family contribution** (or, as noted earlier, the student aid index, the estimate that may soon replace the EFC)—as well as the components of that package, including loans that will need to be repaid. And as noted in the question on the previous page, by accepting an early decision you'll be losing the ability to compare other offers.

Under extenuating circumstances, a college may allow an applicant accepted under an early decision plan to be released from that commitment for financial reasons. The early decision agreement on the Common Application includes this passage: "Should a student who applies for financial aid not be offered an award that makes attendance possible, the student may decline the offer of admission and be released from the Early Decision commitment."

But we caution that you, like the colleges, should enter into such an agreement in good faith—informed, perhaps, by the data generated by the institution's net price calculator, the web tool that each institution provides so that you can estimate your family's potential financial commitment.

In addition to finances, some readers may have two other overarching questions about early decision: Is it to my child's strategic advantage to apply to a particular institution early decision? And what are the risks?

If your child believes that this institution aligns well with what they are seeking to get out of a college experience, then there is an important fact we wish to impart: admission rates under early decision plans are generally higher than in the regular round.

Among the reasons why:

As a former dean of admissions at a university with an early decision plan, Eric considers candidates in this pool to be somewhat self-selecting. Their academic credentials tend to be highly competitive nationally and internationally, and through their application—as well as by their willingness to make a binding commitment—they are signaling their belief that the institution represents a strong match.

More broadly, the University of Pennsylvania and other colleges and universities with early decision plans use them to meet some of their stated institutional goals and priorities, which can also impact admission rates. Recruited student athletes tend to be in this pool, as are legacy candidates.

The early decision pool is typically much smaller than in the regular round. At the University of Pennsylvania, for example, roughly one in seven applicants for the Class of 2024 applied early. Early decision is certainly not without its passionate critics, including those who point out that candidates often come from families of greater privilege—as indicated by the level of education and wealth—which can translate into the ability to afford test prep and other coaching throughout the process. For many of these students and families, the question is often not whether to apply early decision, but where. In some private schools and wealthy suburban public school districts, families may regard an early decision application as a card that must be played lest their child face a disadvantage in the main round.

To readers who may be having similar thoughts, we have one overriding caution: your child just might get in—and that might not be the best outcome, if the question of whether it is the best option for your child was not factored in. In other words, don't let strategy supersede a thoughtful and reflective discovery and search process.

Regardless of your family's background—legacy or first generation, full financial aid or full pay—our hope is that the information and advice we've provided thus far will serve to inform an applicant's decision of whether to avail themselves of an early decision plan.

If that answer is yes, then your child may be ready to push "submit."

If the answer is no, or not sure, then let's consider whether your child might be better off submitting an application under one of the other early application plans.

For those students who want to get an early indication of at least some of their college options without boxing themselves in, early action or rolling admission may provide viable choices.

The questions we posed above regarding early decision can also provide a rigorous framework for evaluating these other options. For example, having an offer in hand before January 1 (or a denial or deferral) can help shape the remainder of your child's application list—and prompt adjustments. An early denial from a college or university that your child felt was firmly in their sweet spot—or maybe even a likely—will mean that some colleges need to be added to the list and perhaps others removed.

Our strong advice here is not to panic, but for your child (perhaps in partnership with you) to take a fresh look at their list, bearing in mind any decisions already received. This may result in a follow-up conversation about risk tolerance and perhaps the shifting of some schools within categories, such as from sweet spot to aspirational.

What about students whose early application has been deferred, or rolled over, for consideration in the main admissions round? In all likelihood that deferral will be accompanied by specific instructions from the admissions office about next steps. These might include a request for a letter from your child, to be submitted through their portal, providing updates on any academic achievements or other accomplishments since they filed their early application. We recommend that this letter be submitted no later than mid-January. Your child should also confirm with their high school that it is sending an updated midyear report that includes their latest grades.

Let's return, for a moment, to the prospect of securing an acceptance under an early action or rolling plan, which can serve to give your child confidence and peace of mind. For those who are interested in receiving an early signal—without the pressure of an immediate commitment—single choice or restrictive early action, if offered at a school of interest, could be an appropriate path. This option may be especially appealing to students who want to have another financial aid offer for comparison—which, in addition to the early action school, could include offers from public universities. Applicants should be aware that the few colleges or universities with single choice or restrictive early action plans are among the most selective in the nation.

Is there a strategic advantage to applying early action, whether restricted or unrestricted, compared to in a school's regular round? Although admission rates may be higher under an early action plan than regular decision—for some of the reasons cited earlier regarding the characteristics of the pool—families should be careful not to conclude from those figures that it is easier to get in early. The main advantage for families is having a decision earlier in the calendar.

We want to close this section with a word about early decision II, the second round of binding early decision, but with later deadlines. Each year, it seems, a growing number of colleges and universities are offering this option. But which students should seriously consider applying EDII?

One group includes those who received a denial in the first round of early decision or early action from another institution. Others may have been told that their application has been deferred to the next round of admission decision-making for further consideration in the larger applicant pool. With that knowledge, a student may look to another top choice on their list that fully aligns with their interests and objectives and, if it has an EDII option, choose to exercise it.

An applicant who may have been deferred, early, at their first-choice college, may come to the conclusion that their prospects of admission are better at another school on their list that offers EDII.

But remember that this is a binding commitment, and your child should feel confident that they would be happy to attend if admitted.

(G.) The Fifth C Revisited: Managing Cost and Affordability

While your child is working on their applications, they will require your assistance to answer some basic questions around the financing of their higher education.

The first question relates to the application itself: Does the school require an application fee, and if so, will your child be requesting a waiver?

While some colleges or universities do not have a fee for submitting and processing an application, others may charge in the range of twenty-five to one hundred dollars. Those that do charge will include a place, such as in the personal profile of the Common Application, where a student can request a fee waiver. Among the factors that colleges consider in granting those waivers are whether your child has received a fee waiver on the SAT or ACT; whether they qualify for a free or reduced-price school lunch; or whether you or your child believe the fee would be burdensome. Your college counselor may also be asked to document that need.

If your child is going to be requesting financial aid from the college or university to which they are applying, you and they are likely going to have to fill out several forms. They will include the **FAFSA**, the Free Application for Federal Student Aid; the **CSS Profile** (from the College Scholarship Service), which is used by private colleges and universities for consideration of nongovernment aid; and sometimes the institution's own financial aid form.

Each of these documents may be required for the granting of

need-based aid, which will be determined by your family's resources, including annual family income and assets. Some institutions may also use the forms as part of the process for determining merit aid, which will be directly related to your child's academic or other achievements and talents.

Following is a brief word about each of those forms, along with some suggestions on instructional resources that you and your child might find helpful.

FAFSA

The Free Application for Federal Student Aid (FAFSA) can be submitted as early as October 1 of your child's senior year of high school, and no later than June 30. As always, your child should check the institutional deadlines, as they may vary by school, and include them in their tracker. While there have been efforts over the years to simplify this form, the experience can feel a bit like filing annual federal taxes, so set aside time not only to complete the form but to gather the information you'll need to have on hand. Specifically, have ready the federal tax forms that you submitted—including the 1040 and any schedules attached to it—in the spring of the year when your child was a junior in high school.

The FAFSA is used to determine eligibility for federal grants (such as Pell), work-study (on-campus jobs), and subsidized or unsubsidized loans under the government's Stafford Loan program. Even families that feel certain they will not qualify for need-based aid should still seriously consider filling out the FAFSA. The unsubsidized Stafford Loan, for example, may make available capital for higher-education-related expenses throughout your child's time in college and is not based on need.

The dense ten-page online form includes sections to be completed by your child as well as by you as their parent. Among the questions asked are whether the applicant's parents are married, divorced, or separated; family wages, income, and investments; whether a parent is deceased; and whether the family receives benefits under Medicaid.

The form is intrusive, and as such may present the first time you are discussing these matters in depth with your child. You are in the best position to decide whether you wish to fill out this document together. Regardless, it can provide an opportunity for you and your child to discuss the financial commitment that their education may require and the shared responsibility for that investment. Once they've enrolled, they may even recall these conversations as they weigh whether to get out of bed for that early morning class—not with a sense of guilt about your financial sacrifice (and theirs, too), but with a sense of ownership.

For those readers seeking advice on filling out the FAFSA, we asked Charlie Javice of Frank for a few tips. She suggests the following:

- As you fill out the form initially, answer each question to the best of your ability, including with estimates where necessary, as you can always go back and edit before filing.

- When asked on the FAFSA for the size of your household, make sure you count everyone, including yourself as a parent, as "it has a huge impact on the amount of aid."

- In the section on assets: if you or others in your household have debts or any liabilities, subtract them.

- If you are a homeowner, the primary home in which you reside is not an asset you report on FAFSA.

- For those parents who may not have filed taxes—and there are any number of reasons why that may be the case—you

could still file your FAFSA, though it may be subject to
enhanced verification, including a review of W-2 and 1099
forms generated by an employer or client.

The time it will take you to fill out the FAFSA can vary widely, depending in part on whether you have all the required information at your fingertips and whether it is organized in a way that lets you reference the documents easily. Filing could take as little as a half hour, though realistically you might set aside several hours for the entire task.

Frank also offers a service, for free, in which it will help you populate your FAFSA form using photos of your tax returns sent from your mobile phone. While the site assures users that it employs "bank-level security to protect your information," readers will have to decide for themselves their level of comfort with sharing their most personal data.

CSS Profile

The College Scholarship Service (CSS) Profile is a product of the College Board, the purveyor of the SAT, and does carry a fee: twenty-five dollars to complete and submit to one school, and sixteen dollars for each additional school, though fee waivers are available. It is used by nearly four hundred "colleges, universities, professional schools, and scholarship programs," according to its website, as an additional source of information on awarding financial aid. For international applicants who are not U.S. citizens, the CSS Profile is the primary financial aid application at those institutions that accept it.

Like the FAFSA, the CSS Profile can be filled out as early as October 1 of your child's senior year, though with an earlier closing date—typically the following January through March, depending on the institution. Unlike the FAFSA, the CSS Profile is for aid that is specific to particular institutions, such as grants and scholarships.

Charlie's caution here is that the CSS "really gets into the weeds" and is typically "longer and harder to fill out" than the FAFSA. It asks for many pieces of supplemental information like value of primary homes (and secondary homes, too), as well as brokerage accounts and business assets. The form, and the instructions on it, can be found in the CSS Profile section of the College Board website.

Financial Aid Forms Specific to a College or University

While the FAFSA and CSS Profile are the major foundation on which your child's aid package will be constructed, some colleges and universities—including those that are public—may require the completion of additional forms. Some institutions ask for these forms to cross-check information provided on the others, as well as to gain additional context on your family's financial picture. Again, you and your child will want to pace yourselves, paying close attention to deadlines, which are likely to be firm.

Outside Scholarships

When colleges or universities use the term "outside scholarships," they are referencing financial aid provided from entities beyond the institution. For example, if your child took the PSAT, they will likely qualify for consideration under the National Merit Scholarship Program, which defines itself as an academic competition based, at least in the initial rounds, on your child's scores. In September of their senior year of high school, they will be informed whether they have been designated as a semifinalist, based on a cutoff score that varies by state. The following February, a subset of semifinalists will be designated as finalists.

The path from finalist to National Merit Scholar includes securing a recommendation from the high school principal or designee; a "record of high academic performance in high school"; and submission of a scholarship application. About seventy-six hundred students will ultimately receive scholarships ranging from $500 to $2,500 annually, including from several hundred colleges and businesses.

Your child may also wish to explore whether outside scholarships are available from your employer or a union; from national talent search competitions, such as those administered by organizations like the Gates and Jack Kent Cooke foundations; from the local Veterans of Foreign Wars (VFW) post or other associations; or from community-based organizations. There may also be programs sponsored by your state, such as the Hope Scholarship in Georgia, or a so-called College Promise program in your state or community that might help defray the cost of the first two years of college, particularly community college.

Military veterans and their dependents may qualify for scholarships under the Post-9/11 GI Bill, which could cover tuition and provide annual stipends for books and supplies.

Essays for Scholarship Applications

Some of the outside scholarship applications listed above may include an essay section. The good news for your child is that the basic prompts very likely mirror those used on the Common Application. While some may be tailored, like those in the college supplements, to the particular mission of a foundation or other sponsoring organization, all are likely to touch on basic ground your child has covered before: Why college? What in your background, or your experiences, has shaped the arc of your life? Who has been an influence?

Where possible, you can encourage your child to revisit earlier essays and drafts from the college process and consider repurposing them for the task at hand. There is nothing wrong with their doing so, as long as they read the specific question carefully and ensure they are speaking to it.

As with your child's college applications, they—and where appropriate, you—will want to ensure that all required financial aid documents have not only been submitted, but received. We spoke earlier about application portals that may be used by each college, with specific login credentials. It is likely that through these same portals your child and you can keep track of the documents received and follow up on those that may be missing.

(H.) Some Thoughts on Pacing, Time Management, and the Parallel Universe Where Life in High School Goes On

The journey on which we have led you and your child in this chapter has been especially intense and probably exhausting. As your child enters the stage where application deadlines are beginning to loom, both of you should take a moment to pause and breathe, and to acknowledge that you have accomplished a lot.

There is, of course, much work still to be done, but happily, there are also natural breaks throughout your child's fall school calendar, and you want to make sure that they take advantage of these opportunities—whether to catch up or get ahead on their college applications or, perhaps, to catch up on some much-needed rest or schoolwork on which they might have fallen behind. You might also take a moment to check in with younger siblings—and, if relevant, your spouse or another partner—to take the measure of how everyone is feeling.

For the last few weeks and months leading up to the final application deadlines, pacing and spacing will be critical. If your child will allow you to play such a role, you might offer yourself up as something of an executive coach—not to plan this frenetic period of their lives, but to help them create some interim deadlines and milestones throughout the concluding stretch.

If they have four, five, six, or more applications due on or around January 1, they should not regard that date as the equivalent of a final exam for which they can cram. Rather, they should create, perhaps with your help, realistic mini-deadlines on which they commit to have certain applications, or at least large portions of them, completed. Encourage them to put those dates on the calendar and in the college application requirement and deadline tracker from Activity #6.

Be on the lookout for the telltale signs of procrastination and avoidance. Often, these behaviors may be rooted not in laziness but in any number of fears—feelings that you or another trusted adult or friend might seek to draw out. Your willingness to listen, without interruption or judgment, is key—as is your willingness to offer encouragement, and perhaps some suggestions, borne from your own experience, on managing a seemingly never-ending to-do list of complex tasks and projects.

As you both populate and revise their fall calendar, your child could assemble a final checklist that is similar to the one we suggested earlier in this section for submitting early applications.

Their final checklist for the submission of applications under the regular decision process might include the following tasks:

- **Print out each application** for one final, proofreading review. A spelling or grammatical error, or an omitted word, which their eye might glance over on a screen, may reveal itself on the printed page.

- Jacques, drawing on his experience as a writer, suggests that for the essay in particular your child **give those sections a series of final reads**, each of them serving a different objective. They should use one read to ensure they have varied their choices of words and have not been repetitive. Another read—and this one can be aloud—would be to check that no sentence is too long, and that the reader has a chance quite literally to take a breath. With a final read, they can focus on whether their main ideas are conveyed clearly. This is not a time to second-guess the topic or approach. Instead, what we are recommending here is a polish.

- **Make sure standardized test scores have been self-reported** in the application **or sent directly** from the testing agencies, depending on the school's policies.

- **Determine whether a fee waiver is being sought.** If not, make sure that your child has access to a credit card or other accepted form of payment.

- **Confirm that recommendations, transcripts, and other supporting materials** from your school have been requested by your child, bearing in mind that your child may need to check in occasionally to make sure these materials have been submitted.

- If applicable, be sure that art, music, or other **portfolios or supplemental materials are ready** for upload.

- **Prioritize those applications that have to be submitted early**, including those your child may be considering submitting for early decision II.

- **Don't wait until the last minute to submit.** We suggest at least a forty-eight-hour buffer prior to any deadline. This is especially important from a technological point of view: systems can crash, electricity can go out, and your home internet can go dark.

As your child runs through this checklist for each of the colleges to which they intend to apply, encourage them to take breaks at strategic and regular moments. They should draw some confidence from the fact that at this stage they remain very much in control of the college process.

You surely know from your own life and work that fatigue can lead to errors and frustration, as well as inefficiency. A cup of coffee with friends, a movie, a nap, or time to just do nothing can be rejuvenating. This free time is a necessity, not a luxury—and certainly not time that your child should feel guilty about allowing themselves. This all falls into the category of self-care.

Potential opportunities to take a break are complicated by the fact that life in school goes on—with papers due, exams scheduled, and homework pressing. Those deadlines, too, might be logged on the master calendar so that your child, and you, can have a full view of these multiple and competing demands.

(I.) Ready to Submit

And now the time is at hand. Your child is ready to press "submit." And so they do.

They may experience a range of emotions, whether immediately or a day or so later. You, as a parent, should keep an eye and ear out for signals of how they are feeling. They might be elated and relieved that the task at hand is complete. Or they may feel a sudden letdown, having pushed for months, if not years, to get to this point. They may start second-guessing themselves—whether over their choice of schools or over an idea expressed in an essay.

Your job is to be supportive and reassuring and to help them begin to let go and to move on with their lives. This may also be a teaching opportunity, where you can help your child take their eyes off the rearview mirror, as well as their gaze off the road far ahead, and perhaps pull off to the side of that road. The aim is for them to be present in the current moment—maybe for the first time in a long while. Give them some advice, if they are willing to hear it, about how to prepare themselves for what is likely to be a long wait.

A college decision is not a package delivered the next day by Amazon Prime. Waiting is hard, particularly for this digital generation, and you may need to assist them with strategies for shifting gears.

Over these next few days and weeks, encourage your child to slip back into a more regular routine, one that is less frenetic than in the previous weeks and months. While they still have to maintain their grades, their schedules should open up—providing them time for a return to something resembling normalcy. For the first time in a long time, they can take control of their own calendars, with the intention of reconnecting with those things that give them joy.

You're also surely experiencing your own strong feelings, so give yourself the opportunity to step back, take stock, and recharge. Amid the final frenzy of the application process, you may have unintentionally neglected yourself or others in your life. Now can be the time to reorient and focus on other priorities.

Months from now, a new series of decisions about the college process will be arrayed in front of you and your child. But the last of your child's college applications going out the door is most certainly a milestone. And it is a milestone that we hope you, as a parent, will acknowledge and celebrate.

PART IV

*Conversations About
the Decisions*

(A.) Back Inside the Admissions Office: Conversations About the Applicants, and Building a Class

Up until this point in the College Conversation, the responsibility for decision-making, and the control of that process, has largely rested with your child and you. While the rules of engagement are established by the colleges and universities, your child had a fair amount of latitude throughout the processes of discovery, search, and application. Now that your child has pressed "submit," the responsibility for decision-making shifts to the admissions committees of the schools to which they have applied.

In this regard, the American college admissions process is unique when compared to much of the rest of the world. Across much of Europe and Asia, for example, college placement is a centralized function carried out by a national government or ministry. Sometimes opportunities are restricted, as in Great Britain, where a student can apply to Oxford or Cambridge, but not to both, at least not in the same year. (Imagine how such constraints would play in the United States.) Meanwhile, in China, the National College Entrance Examination, also known as Gaokao, is the sole determinant for whether someone attends a university, and if so, which one.

While the American college admissions process may be maddening—and even inscrutable—to many because of its lack of predictability, it does provide students and families with a degree of flexibility and choice that would be inconceivable in other parts of the world. Which isn't to say that it's not stressful for applicants and their parents.

If you will indulge our returning to the automobile analogy: when last we left you and your child, having just pushed "submit," you had effectively pulled your car into a rest area. But rather than turn the engine off, you might more appropriately keep it idling. That's because it's now time for your child to begin accessing the colleges' admissions portals and monitoring whether each institution has received test scores, recommendations, and transcripts, in addition to the components of each application. Checking email regularly for reminders or notifications is also important.

How often should your child (in partnership with you, if they like) log in to the portal to track receipt of all necessary materials? A good rule of thumb is to check once a week for the first few weeks after the application deadline. If any item is missing, your child may want to talk with the person or entity responsible for submitting it. If a standardized test score has not been received, they may need to reach out to the College Board or ACT. For a transcript, they should check in with their college counselor. If they are told that these items were submitted long ago, then they should reach out to the admissions office, usually through a designated email address. Picking up the phone should not be the first step taken, but if a matter cannot be resolved by email, then a student should, by all means, call the admissions office.

Other than keeping track of submissions, your child has no other role to play during this phase of the decision process—other than, of course, to maintain a strong and engaged performance in high school, and to savor these final months of their high school experience.

For those parents who may be wondering what happens to an application from the time your child submits it to the moment that they log in to their portal for a decision, we'll spend some time in the following pages describing the process.

Back when you may have been applying to college, you dropped your paperwork in the mail, and it eventually made its way to an admissions office mailroom, where literally hundreds of bins of similar submissions would be sorted and organized into files with color-coded tabs, to be piled high, eventually, on an admissions officer's desk. It was a manually intensive process, and the weeks that it took just to open and move the mail left less time for the evaluation and selection of the candidates.

As a first-year admissions officer at the University of Pennsylvania in 1987, from mid-January to mid-March, Eric evaluated more than 1,000 applications from across the Commonwealth of Pennsylvania, which was part of his designated region. His territory also included applicants from the Carolinas and Indiana. Typically, it took him an hour to read 4 to 5 applications, which translated to about 25 applications a day, and perhaps 150 or more in a week (including weekends), for the better part of eight weeks. Much of his reading was done at home, which meant toting piles of folders to and from the office. In each instance, as he moved from a student's paper transcript to letters of recommendations to essays, he took notes on a triplicate form. Those entries would include ratings for each applicant—in categories both academic and personal—that would eventually be collected by another team and then entered into a mainframe computer.

This was merely the first step in a process that could include a review of the application by a second reader, as well as perhaps a subcommittee and even the committee of the whole. That year, the University of Pennsylvania received nearly 13,000 applications and offered acceptance to about 4,600, for an admission rate of roughly 35 percent, to enroll a class of more than 2,000 students.

Today, when your child presses "submit," the bits and bytes of their application traverse thousands of miles in an instant and land in a digital queue housed in the cloud, ready for review by the admissions office once most elements of the application have been received and compiled. All the time that was once spent sorting can now be dedicated to the review of applications. Yet over the last three decades, the volume of applications may have doubled or tripled at places like the University of Pennsylvania—which means there are many more applications to review in that same relatively short period of time.

In recent years, when Eric and his colleagues reviewed an application, they did so in the office, with dual-screen monitors connected to their laptops. Rather than being sequestered alone, each admissions officer evaluated an application while sitting next to an admissions colleague, their initial impressions recorded not in triplicate but with a few keystrokes.

Earlier, we advised that your child should consider reading their essay aloud. In addition to proofreading, one of the reasons we encourage this practice is that the two (or more) admissions officers considering your child's application may well read key passages out loud to each other. This process, known as committee-based evaluation, was introduced several years ago at the University of Pennsylvania and has since been adopted at several dozen other highly selective institutions.

An initial evaluation that used to take Eric fifteen minutes alone can now be accomplished, in tandem, in five. Working together as a team, each can highlight for the other aspects of an application that stood out. Moreover, the time saved by admissions officers at this stage of the process, compared to years past, is considered crucial by proponents of committee-based evaluation, enabling others responsible for admission decisions as well as key partners across campus (including faculty and academic advisers) to be involved as well. At the University of Pennsylvania, for example, which received more than 42,000 applications for the Class of 2024, Eric and more than thirty other colleagues worked at a pace of about 12 applications an hour (nearly 100 a day, and 500 to 600 a week).

Some parents may be unnerved by the notion of two people who have probably never met their child making a preliminary recommendation about them in just five minutes. When Jacques spent the 1999–2000 academic year as an observer in the admissions office at another selective school, Wesleyan University in Connecticut, as part of the reporting for his book *The Gatekeepers: Inside the Admissions Process of a Premier College*, the admissions officers individually devoted at least twenty minutes to their initial consideration of each application, which were then still submitted on paper. And indeed, the admissions officers at many highly selective schools—including some as highly selective as the University of Pennsylvania—still do. For his part, Eric argues that, like a workout at the gym, the intensity and quality of time spent on the review may outweigh the quantity, particularly if an officer is paired with a partner.

Regardless of the time they spend initially on each application, admissions officers generally seek the same qualities in an applicant—

and a class—that they have for the past three decades. We discussed earlier that most four-year colleges and universities use some variation of the holistic admissions process, which values the whole person, including the courses they took (and the rigor of those courses); their grades; their recommendations; their activities and their commitment to those activities; and the ideas expressed through their essays and interviews. It is the interplay of these elements, as opposed to one overriding factor, that an admissions officer will consider.

Earlier we mentioned the concept of demonstrated interest. This is the metric that some colleges use to help predict whether an applicant is likely to enroll if admitted, as gauged through their attendance at recruitment events, whether at their high school or on campus, as well as their online engagement, including through their opening of electronic communications.

You may be asking yourself: Does such a show of commitment really matter? Depending on the college, if an acceptance decision is considered close in the eyes of the admissions office, then demonstrated interest might well make a difference. Our advice is that if a college or university made it onto your child's list, then they should continue to be attentive to any communication and outreach from the admissions office during this decision phase. This also includes being responsive to any outreach from alumni volunteers who are setting up interviews.

So how, then, does an institution like the University of Pennsylvania consider tens of thousands of applications—most from students who are highly qualified—and winnow them to just a few thousand offers of admission? In some respects, their process is not unlike the one engaged in by you and your child in making their college choices. Your child had the opportunity to consider a few thousand four-year colleges and universities, to yield a list that might range from four to perhaps a dozen. And, to continue the analogy, if you and your child assembled that list using only the *U.S. News & World Report* rankings, that narrow list would probably look far more different, and far less thoughtful and interesting, than the roster your child ultimately compiled.

If admissions officers merely crunched applicants' grade point averages, class ranks, and test scores, the resulting class would also be far less interesting and engaging. Using those metrics, that class would also not be broadly representative of an applicant pool that—at the University of Pennsylvania, for example—draws from more than ten thousand high schools (more than double that of a generation ago), from all fifty states, and more than one hundred countries. As these figures suggest, over the course of the last three decades many colleges and universities have gone from being local to national to international institutions, while the size of their first-year classes have largely remained the same.

This is among the reasons that the University of Pennsylvania is one of several dozen highly selective colleges and universities with an admission rate that has dropped to single digits in recent years. After going through the admissions process, you may well hear an observation from other parents along the lines of, "I can't believe no one from our high school got admitted to," and here you can fill in the name of the highly selective college or university of your choice. We made the point earlier in this book that most of the nation's colleges and universities offer admission to the majority of students who apply—which is why we recommended that your child assemble a balanced list consistent with our concept of admissions alignment.

A college's overarching objective is to ensure that the first-year community as a whole encompasses students with a range of academic and intellectual interests, from the humanities to the social sciences to the natural sciences, as well as, in the case of many universities, professional programs like business, engineering, and nursing. An admissions officer's job is not merely to ensure there is a critical mass of students interested in a particular department or major, though this is an important consideration. Just as your child sized up potential colleges and universities, at least in part, based on the sports, clubs, and activities offered, admissions officers also consider how an applicant will participate in, and ultimately lead, those activities on their campuses. Those include intercollegiate sports teams, orchestras, a cappella groups, countless student publications, and student government.

Most colleges and universities are also committed to cultivating first-year communities that are broadly diverse—encompassing students' racial and socioeconomic backgrounds; whether they would be the first in their families to attend college; how they identify in terms of gender and, if they reference it, sexual orientation; and where they grew up, not just geographically but whether in small towns or big cities. Creating a community is a particular priority for institutions that are primarily residential, and where learning often occurs far from the classroom in dormitories, libraries, dining halls, and other environments.

Many colleges and universities will, as discussed earlier in this book, also give special consideration to students whose parents and perhaps grandparents attended that institution. Among the reasons these institutions may do so is in recognition of a family's long-standing connection to, and support of, their alma mater, which they may have expressed by volunteering their time or through philanthropic donations. This practice has long been under fire as perpetuating privilege. But a student's legacy status continues to be among the many factors that can matter in the admissions process, though it is well short of a guarantee of admission.

Is the process we have described over the last few pages fair? The two of us are not here to argue whether it is or not. But what would a process that *is* fair look like?

That depends in part on your definition of merit. Would it be based exclusively on standardized test scores?

Those tempted to say yes should bear in mind that students' performance on such tests correlate, at least in part, to their parents' level of education, as well as their ability to access and afford test prep.

If you consider instead a definition of merit that encompasses high school grades and class rank, as evaluated in a vacuum, then some account must be taken of the vast disparity in resources and funding across K-12 education in this country. To level the playing field, admissions officers attempt to look at an applicant within the context of the environment in which they grew up.

But could the admissions process be made more fair? A number of academics, as well as college counselors and admissions officers themselves, are raising that very question—and seeking to provide answers.

In November 2019, a grassroots collective of admissions professionals that calls itself ACCEPT (Admissions Community Cultivating Equity and Peace Today) convened admissions officers, college counselors, nonprofit leaders, and others for a two-day gathering in Washington, DC, called Hack the Gates. (The "gates" refer to the admissions offices that serve as a metaphorical entryway to every college and university.)

The group met "to facilitate a national, evidence-based dialogue" with two main objectives: "to critically analyze systemic pathways and barriers in college admissions, particularly for students of color and low-income students" as well as "to generate and identify innovative and transformative potential solutions to remove barriers and inequities in college admissions."

As a series of racially motivated hate crimes drew national attention and protest, the admissions profession accelerated its review of policies and practices as viewed through these lenses. Meanwhile, a series of cases, including those challenging affirmative action, were making their way through various levels of the U.S. judicial system.

While these important conversations and deliberations continue, and may well lead to fundamental changes in the admissions process in the not-too-distant future, your child's decision will still likely be made through the processes we described earlier in this section.

After weighing, debating, and often agonizing over each decision, as winter gives way to spring, admissions officers will finally call time.

Using the University of Pennsylvania, once again, as an example of a highly selective institution, consider the statistics for those offered admission in the undergraduate Class of 2023: 16 percent qualified for the Pell Grant, one measure of a low-income background; 51 percent self-identified as students of color; 15 percent were first generation; 16 percent were international; 53 percent were female; 17 percent were legacies; 9 percent were recruited student athletes. The SAT scores of the middle 50 percent, those whose scores ranked from the twenty-fifth to the seventy-fifth percentile, ranged from 1460 to 1550 (out of 1600), and ACT scores ranged from 33 to 35 (out of 36); nearly 96 percent graduated in the top 10 percent of their high school classes; and the mean grade point average of a student offered admission to the class was 3.9 (on an unweighted 4.0 scale).

This snapshot of an admitted class hardly tells the full story at the University of Pennsylvania or any other four-year institution, as it doesn't even begin to capture the voices and experiences and perspectives of the individuals who submitted applications. It does, however, provide an indication of at least some of the factors that are taken into consideration in the admissions process.

And with that, it is the admissions office's turn to push "submit"—typically throughout March and into early April. Via their portals they will issue admission decisions for applicants to the incoming first-year class: admit, deny, or a spot on the waiting list.

(B.) Back to the Kitchen Table: Sorting, Weighing, and Analyzing the Colleges' Decisions

If you're the parent of a high school senior, April is likely to be a hectic month. As you and your child are anticipating those college decisions, you might want to take a moment, in advance, to look at calendars.

Throughout April most colleges are going to have **admitted student days** (and possibly overnights and weekends, when possible), as well as virtual outreach through social media and webinars, to enable your child to gather more information so that they can make a final decision. These events are also referred to as "yield days," as colleges embark on the process of "converting" admitted students to students who will put down a deposit, with the intention to enroll.

The challenge, of course, is that as winter gives way to spring, your child may not yet know whether these dates are relevant—in other words, have they been admitted?—and the colleges themselves will likely not have announced those dates until the decision has been released.

Which means you need to do some prior planning, without

having the exact details in hand. There are, however, some things you do know.

For example, working with your April calendar—whether online or on hard copy—you should note religious or cultural holidays. To the extent that Easter or Passover falls in April during a given year, this may not be the year to buy advance, nonrefundable tickets to travel across the country to visit family. Most colleges will try to avoid scheduling admitted student programming on Good Friday, Easter Sunday, or the first night of Passover—but contiguous days are likely fair game. We also wish to gently remind you of another annual rite in the month of April: Tax Day. This is probably not the year to procrastinate completing those 1040 forms.

You might also include in your April calendar those dates when you as a parent don't have the flexibility to travel, whether because of work commitments or the needs of other family members, as well as when your child has responsibilities they absolutely can't miss or reschedule. The high school calendar, of course, continues on—and depending where in the country you are, these could be among the final weeks of high school. Finally, we suggest that you make note on your calendar of the last few days in April, leading up to May 1, which is the date that many colleges continue to observe as the deadline for accepted students to declare where they intend to enroll. As you will see a bit later, our counsel is that your child not wait until the final minutes of April 30 to push "submit" on that decision. That said, you as a parent will likely want to be around in those days leading up to May 1, to be supportive and to be a sounding board. Indeed, you as a family may have some financial decisions to make during this time.

We'll revisit the subject of admitted student days in a few pages, at the point that your child has a more concrete sense of their options. And we'll include in that part of *The College Conversa-*

tion suggestions for how to discuss whether or when you might accompany your child to an admitted student day (which may also have a parent component), and also ways your child might balance those visits with other priorities in and out of school. At this point, all we are suggesting is that you take control of what you know, understanding that you may need to keep your calendar as clear as possible.

Those of you who received your own college decisions via the U.S. mail—in the days when a fat packet might signal acceptance and a thin envelope denial (or an offer to join the waiting list)—will recall that those envelopes may have landed in your mailbox sporadically, over the course of several days and possibly weeks. No admissions office could tell applicants exactly when decision letters would be delivered.

Today, each college will name a specific date on which they intend to release decisions. Depending on the school, the range of possible dates can extend over multiple weeks, from mid-March to early April. Within that period there will be days on which certain colleges will cluster. For example, the eight institutions of the Ivy League will release their regular decision results on the same day and at the same time, usually in the last few days of March. For some colleges the particular day has special meaning and serves as a reflection of the institution's culture. At the Massachusetts Institute of Technology, for example, admission decisions have historically been released on March 14, which is known as Pi Day. Those of you with even a rudimentary memory of high school math will recall that pi rounds to 3.14. MIT actually takes that math lesson a step further and typically releases decisions at 6:28 p.m., Eastern time, mindful that 6.28 (or double the value of pi) is known as tau.

Your child will likely be notified a few weeks in advance when decisions are being released. Here, too, we advise putting key dates and times on their calendars, as well as their tracking grids. If a college hasn't indicated when it will be sending out notifications, your child or their college counselor should feel free to call the admissions office to ask if that date has been established.

A number of applicants to some colleges and universities may have already received notification earlier in the admissions process indicating a high probability of their acceptance, a document known as a **likely letter.** One such category of recipients includes recruited student athletes, who are often pressed by college coaches to make a decision about which school they will attend. Other such letters will be sent to applicants whom the colleges or universities consider to be a high priority for acceptance, based on their academic achievement, intellectual interests, and, perhaps, unique talents. Given that the number of applicants who receive these letters is relatively small, your child should not handicap their chances of admission based on whether such a letter arrives.

For most institutions, the final admission decision will appear in those portals where your child has been tracking the receipt of their application materials, which means that they'll need their login credentials to learn their results. A few institutions do still mail their decisions and will likely acknowledge online, prior to the mailing date, when they will do so. Even those colleges that use the portal to issue decisions will still send thick acceptance packets of printed material, usually arriving a few days later, which will include a formal decision letter along with other important documents, including those for financial aid.

As these notification dates approach, you might want to engage your child in a conversation about how and where they wish to receive the news, and whether they want you close by. There are certainly no absolute rules here, but be aware that these moments can be emotionally fraught, with months and sometimes years of built-up anticipation. Bear in mind your child's temperament, and how they process disappointment—as well as elation or uncertainty.

Depending on where in the country (or the world) you reside, the decision may arrive in the middle of a workday or even the middle of the night. If a college is pushing out tens of thousands of notifications simultaneously, it has to ensure proper staffing, including seeing to it that their IT teams are on hand in the event of a glitch. For this reason many colleges tend to release results between three p.m. and seven p.m. in their own time zone.

But assuming your child wants you present when they receive news of a decision, what should your role be? If you're both inclined to have your role be that of the house photographer or videographer charged with documenting the moment, be prepared for any possibility. Whatever you decide, remember that you have the long perspective of an adult who has experienced life in all its complexity, including any number of disappointments as well as moments of celebration. Bring that perspective to help your child process whatever results they receive.

As noted earlier, the decisions a college issues in the regular round are yes, no, and maybe (in the case of the waiting list). In many instances, those decisions will arrive on separate days and on the colleges' timelines. But if multiple decisions are coming on the same day, your child might want to give thought as to whether they have a preference about which school they would like to check first. They might wish to revisit their thoughtfully constructed college list and establish an order from those institutions they handicapped as likely, in the sweet spot, or aspirational. If your child constructed a balanced list, along the lines that we've encouraged throughout *The College Conversation*, we hope that they've received an acceptance from at least one of the institutions they considered to be likely. If that's the case, we also hope that institution is one that your child is genuinely enthusiastic to attend. Any other acceptances will only give them further choices to consider.

If your child received a denial from any of the schools on their list, and especially those that they most wanted to attend, emotions may be running high. While you may understand that this is not a life-or-death moment, you can appreciate that it may feel that way to your child. Give them the space and the time to have those feelings, and to share them with you when they're ready. Simply listening or responding with a hug or other gesture of consolation may be all that your child needs in that moment. Sometimes your mere presence will be enough. Recognize that as with so many other events in life, they're going to be observing you closely, looking for signs that all will be fine and that you're not disappointed in them.

Don't be surprised if you find yourself recalling other moments throughout their young lives when they experienced rejection or sadness. While a low grade on a term paper, a fall on the ice in a skating competition, or the breakup of a close friendship are on a different order of magnitude than a college decision, you'll likely frame the latter in a similar perspective, confident that their hurt feelings will indeed pass. Recognize, though, that perspective may be of little comfort to them in the moment.

You also have to consider your own emotions. Your natural response as a parent to a college or university that denied your child acceptance—including, perhaps, one that you attended—may well be anger. Going into protective mode, leavened with a bit of fight-or-flight response, your first impulse might be to shoot off an angry email to the dean of admissions or to pick up the phone to protest what you might regard as an injustice. Resist any urge to lash out.

It may be small comfort, but remember that this process is not predictable, and it should never be viewed as a report card on your parenting or your child's self-worth. Whatever judgments are made in the admissions process are ultimately subjective and human. In the coming days, we hope that your child and you will be able to step back and weigh those decisions that were a source of disappointment against the acceptances from other institutions. We'll have more to say on how to weigh those options a bit later.

When the news is good, follow the wise advice of Eileen Cunningham Feikens, the dean of college counseling at Dwight-Englewood School in New Jersey, who urges students and families alike to "celebrate with dignity." That means avoiding the inclination—however well-intentioned—for you or your child to share the good news on any acceptances immediately on social media. Friends, teammates, and classmates who applied to the same institution may have received less favorable news, and you should be sensitive to that. Your child may also wish to avoid the temptation to wear that institution's sweatshirt to school the next day. Many schools will designate a day later in the school year when its graduating students may wear their new colors with pride.

For parents whose children were the recipients of good news, don't be surprised if a moment of letdown follows. After crossing the finish line following months of preparation and up to seventeen hours of continuous exercise and exertion, many Ironman triathletes have been surprised to feel a sensation best characterized as anticlimactic. Whether you're an elite endurance athlete or an elite college applicant, you can sometimes become lulled by the belief that life will instantly be different and better once a herculean goal has been achieved. But as adults and parents, we know better: our children are still the same people they were even moments before their accomplishment was realized. Sometimes that reality can be a bit deflating. All of which gives you as a parent yet another teaching moment.

For those applicants offered a spot on the waiting list, this may feel like the college admissions version of limbo. In reality there is no list—at least not one in ranked order, as if it were a queue for purchasing tickets outside a theater. Instead, applicants who have been asked whether they wish to continue to have their applications considered, should spaces in the incoming class become available in the coming months, are placed in a pool. Whether the college ultimately draws from that pool will depend on any number of factors.

One is a function of capacity—namely, the number of spaces left after students who are offered acceptance say yes in response. If the college overshoots its **yield**, which is the percentage of students offered admission who say yes, and has more students in the first-year class than desired, then the institution likely will not go to its waiting list at all. But if, after all the results are tallied, there is room in the first-year class, a college admissions office might offer a spot in that class for a number of different reasons.

If, for example, the incoming first-year class at an institution's engineering school is a bit short, then an admissions office might offer a seat to someone on the waiting list who specifically applied to that school or program. When there is space in the class, and room to take at least some students off the waiting list, colleges may also weigh and consider those institutional priorities discussed earlier, including the area of the country or world from which a student is applying; whether they are first generation or a Pell Grant recipient; or whether they have expressed interest in studying in a department where interest is light thus far in the incoming first-year class.

How many students might be placed on a waiting list—and how many of them might then be offered places in the class—can vary widely by institution and year. The rough percentage of those put on the list might be equivalent to the school's overall admission rate. So, if a college offers admission to 10 percent of applicants overall, then another 10 percent might find themselves on the waiting list. How many will then be brought into the class? It could be as few as several dozen or as many as several hundred.

We'll have more to say later about how you might discuss with your child whether they wish to remain on a waiting list—and, if so, whether they might share supplemental information, including academic or other updates since they submitted their application. They can take more time, perhaps up to a week, to assemble any supporting material.

Because some college and university admissions offices move very quickly to consider applicants on the waiting list, your child should not hesitate to let an institution know that they wish to confirm their spot on the list—ideally no later than within forty-eight hours of having received notice of that decision. They can likely do so directly through their applicant portal. Confirming interest in continued consideration on the waiting list is a relatively low-risk proposition, as it involves no financial cost.

ⓒ Your Child Is Back in the Driver's Seat, with Decisions to Make

"What do we do now?"

Some readers may be old enough to remember a 1972 Robert Redford movie called *The Candidate*. In it, Redford's character wages an uphill battle to be elected as one of California's two United States senators—and, somehow and to his own surprise, he wins. Which prompts him to utter that question.

You may be hearing similar questions in your own home, considering that, as in an election, so much of your child's energy was likely concentrated on the ultimate outcome. They may have considered getting into college, or a series of colleges, to be the equivalent of reaching that finish line or emerging victorious from a campaign. But they may not have given much thought to what comes next, including sorting through more than a few options. While that is understandable, the decision deadline looms, which means that it is once again time to get grounded so that they might make an informed decision.

Within a few days of your child's having received the last of their admission decisions, with the exception of any that may be pending via the waiting list, they will want to begin the process of taking stock of where they stand, as well as establishing the criteria for how they will make a final decision. They will also want to determine any additional information they need to gather, including through campus visits.

But first, as your child draws you into their decision-making process—and we hope they do—you might consider reminding them how they reached this point and how they might assess whether their thinking has changed. And if so, why?

All the materials that they, with your help, have prepared through the activities in this book are worth gathering and re-examining now. In that initial index card, your child sketched the rough characteristics of their college environment, as did you. Through the self-reflection of the discovery process that yielded their Five I's, they produced an inventory of their identity, intellect, ideas, interests, and inspiration. They then aligned those aspects of themselves with the comparable attributes of the colleges and universities that would end up on their lists, those institutions' Four C's—culture, curriculum, community, and conclusions—as well as the fifth C, cost.

As your child collects this material, they might put it to use in an activity that will frame this next and final phase of the decision process. One goal of this exercise is to guard against snap decisions, which may be based on any number of human emotions, including an understandable desire just to be done. While your child doesn't have a lot of time, they likely have the better part of a month for their deliberations, and we want to encourage you to encourage them to use that time wisely.

> ### ACTIVITY #10: Your Child Revisits Their Priorities as the College Choice Looms

For this activity, have your child retrieve their index cards from Activity #1, in which they free-associated their early thinking on the type of college environment they saw themselves in. We suggest they do so with an eye toward validating or updating what matters most to them at this stage of the process. While we are labeling this an activity, it is actually more of a meditation or moment for reflection.

Just as at the beginning of the process, when we advised that your child and you not consider specific colleges and universities, we recommend here that they temporarily put their all their current college options in a drawer, virtual or otherwise, to be consulted shortly.

For now we want them to review what they noted as their priorities and, where necessary, make edits. Six to nine months in the life of a teenager can be a period of intense growth, introspection, and change—so much so that what they valued earlier in the process may not necessarily be the case now, particularly with the prospect of attending college and perhaps leaving home drawing near.

While they may wish to do this activity alone and then review the results with you, you can also launch them with a series of prompts. Among those that you might ask them to bear in mind as they use fresh eyes—and a bit of distance—to review their earlier thinking are those intended to help them refine and prioritize their preferences within the following categories:

- **Environmental:** At this point, how important to you is an institution's size, location, and distance from home, when weighed against other factors? For those who expressed interest in colleges and universities in a city, does that now mean an institution within the city limits, or just access to a city nearby?

- **Academic:** What about your interest in a particular field of study? Is there more than one path to pursuing it (such as the openness of a student interested in biology or chemistry to studying environmental science or earth and oceanographic science), keeping in mind that schools may offer different areas of specialization based on faculty and their research?

- **Student life:** What are those aspects of social life or extracurricular activities that would create an enriching atmosphere and experience outside the classroom?

- **X factor:** What else really matters to you? Is doing nonprofit work a priority, particularly work that would enable you to feel like a member of the community of which the college is a part, as opposed to feeling like a mere tenant or visitor? What about the availability of support services, such as tutoring, counseling, or proximity to specialized medical care? What about the local music or restaurant scene, or whether professional sports teams play nearby?

The completion of this exercise brings us to a critically important activity, one that will take stock of the list of their current college options—yes, they can pull them out of the drawer now—as viewed through the lenses you both have thoughtfully crafted above.

ACTIVITY #11: Mapping the Choice

For this activity, your child will want to create a fresh spreadsheet or handwritten grid laid out horizontally, whether on a piece of legal paper or a whiteboard, with plenty of room for notes. The thought of creating yet another document at this point in the process may leave you feeling a bit fatigued, but as with any of these activities, feel free to do what works best for your child and you—which could well entail some cutting and pasting. But we also want to make the case for a slate that is literally clean and uncluttered, which will best serve clearer decision-making.

Down the left side of the chart write the names of the accepting colleges or universities from which your child is choosing. List them in alphabetical order, so as not to bias the outcome. If relevant, include a second set of schools, again alphabetically, at which they were placed on the waiting list.

Across the top of the grid write the Five C's: culture, curriculum, community, conclusions, and cost. So how should your child fill in those spaces where the college name meets each of the C's? This is where the I's come in: identity, intellect, ideas, interests, and inspiration.

Just to be clear: we don't want them to actually write the Five I's in those spaces but rather their thoughts on how their I's intersect the C's for each institution. For example, let's imagine they are looking at the first school on their list, alphabetically, under the category of curriculum. They might ask themselves how their academic and intellectual interests align with the curricular offerings of this institution and then capture their reflections in that space. This should be a free-flowing exercise, almost meditative, and consist of just words or phrases. Ultimately these reflections are intended as a personal guide for them and you as they measure their choices against one another in a way that is more nuanced than a simple pro/con list.

As another example: How might their interests align with each of the institutions on their list? These could actually be split among several categories. If they are looking to have access to a vibrant Greek life, they might make that notation under culture, community, or both. If it is civic engagement that is a priority, that, too, could be noted under culture and community as well as curriculum. As a parent, working within the boundaries that you established early on, you might want to take note of a school's track record on outcomes—such as graduation rates, graduate school admission rates, and career pathways and placement. These would go under conclusions.

To the extent a school has offered your child need-based or merit-based financial aid, you might want to go so far as to note some of those actual amounts, as well as the anticipated net price under cost. For many families net price will be the determinative factor in making the college choice, which may prove to be a source of tension between you and your child. We will have more to say about the subject of cost later, and will suggest then that you revisit those notations.

In one respect this is very much a cognitive exercise, as your child and you will be recording facts that will inform their decision. But you should also expect this to be a highly emotional undertaking. We want your child to be in tune with how some of the aspects of these particular institutions make them feel. Be on the lookout for any clues and cues from your child, not only in what they're saying but how they're behaving.

You'll recall that very early on, we suggested that you ask your child what factors in the college process might be a source of anxiety. Some of those factors, such as an institution's distance from home and even the prospect of leaving home, might now be bubbling back up to the surface, taking on more immediacy as a final decision looms. Have an honest conversation with your child about any of the elements weighing on that decision that are a source of concern. Listen to and understand not only what they are saying but also what emotions truly lie underneath. Are they feeling generalized unease about this next step in their lives? Or are there attributes of a particular school that are giving them pause?

For now your child might want to note their specific concerns in the most appropriate box on their grid—along with, perhaps, a follow-up question or two that can serve to address the issue, and either affirm or resolve it. Also encourage them to note with a question mark any gaps on the grid where they need more information. For example, if they want to have as much flexibility and choice as possible to select courses outside their major, they can note under the box for curriculum their wish to explore in more depth the extent to which the schools on their list mandate so-called **distribution requirements**. Although these requirements may not be course specific, they will involve modes of thinking and areas of knowledge that the faculty has determined all students must have. Making mandatory a certain number of courses in areas such as the humanities, social sciences, the natural sciences, and quantitative thinking will also help provide some structure to their course schedule.

After raising those aspects of the college experience that may take your child outside their comfort zone, discourage them from simply or conveniently retreating to safer ground. Urge them to embrace the college experience as one of growth, and assure them that a certain amount of anxiety is natural. By listening to and drawing on all that you know about your child, you'll be in a good position to advise them on whether a fear they are expressing is one of the unknown, or a lack of confidence, or something more serious.

One final note of caution: your child may be eager to make a rush to judgment, either because they have strong convictions about their final choice or simply because they want to bring this protracted process to an end. Of course, it is possible that they do know with some degree of confidence which school they wish to attend among the final choices. It could be one that deferred them in the early round and has accepted them now. In such cases, of course, there may be no reason to wait, as long as all the variables or factors align, including the cost of that education and how you and your child will finance it.

But reassure your child that they do have time—in all likelihood the better part of a month—to make a final decision, while being careful to meet any deadlines specific to that institution. Emphasize to them that time, when well used, can often bring clarity. Use this opportunity to engage in your own thoughtful, deliberative decision-making, and share with them the value of taking a break and having some separation and distance from the decision at hand. Time out with friends, exercise, sleep, and meditation can complement the process that will ultimately lead to their final decision and put them (and you) in the best frame of mind to make it.

(D.) Another Round of Due Diligence: Supporting Your Child as They Weigh Their Final Choices

In embarking on a final round of due diligence, you and your child should be aware that they may feel like they're on overload, especially as the colleges and universities that accepted them seek to convince them to accept their offers of admission.

This wooing begins at the very moment an acceptance is delivered through the college's portal, perhaps with its fight song blaring over the computer speakers accompanied by an image of the school mascot. It is all designed to get your child excited.

And then, as soon as the admission decision has been communicated, the college will immediately seek to draw an accepted student into the community by not only asking them if they are ready to commit but also steering them toward decisions they will need to make. These may include joining accepted students' groups on social media and signing up to attend admitted student days.

If possible, advise your child to take advantage of the opportunity to visit—or revisit—the campuses of those institutions that they are seriously considering attending. Even if they have been there several times before, they will view each place through a different lens with the knowledge that the prospect of their attending is now no longer aspirational but real.

For some families this round of in-person due diligence can have financial implications. If this is the case, your child can reach out to the admissions office (or in some cases a local community-based organization that may have supported them through the college process) to see if they might cover at least a portion of the cost of travel, if not all of it.

You as a parent will now likely be feeling your own set of emotions—including, perhaps, your own concerns about your child even visiting a particular campus, let alone moving there. While we acknowledged earlier that such feelings are universal, we also suggested that they may be especially heightened in households where a child going off to college is in the first generation to do so.

Omar Monteagudo, a native of Cuba and the principal of the School for Advanced Studies in Miami we introduced earlier, said that he has made something of a specialty of offering counsel and reassurance to first-generation fathers, and first-generation fathers of daughters in particular.

"The fear is the notion of independence," he explained. "The fear that there will be no one there to respond if something happens, and that you as a parent won't be able to get in the car and drive there, especially if they are going to college so far from their house.

"This notion is in our culture," he added. "You have to stay local. You have to stay close to the family.

"You've hit the lottery," is what he tells anxious parents to reassure them. "You've sacrificed, you came to this country. The question here is, would we want to shortchange your child because of the fact that you are concerned or scared of the uncertainty of sending your child away?

"In many cases, it does the trick," he said, especially when his own messaging is amplified by other first-generation parents whose children went to college far from home in previous years.

At High Tech High in San Diego, we asked Chloe Rodriguez, a student who prevailed on her mother to allow her to attend New York University in New York City, what advice she would give to first-generation parents like her mom who might be resistant to their child's moving away.

"I would just say you have to trust in your kid," she said. "I mean, they love you. You love them. And if something happens, there's always a way to communicate."

Have an open conversation with your child about their feelings—and yours—concerning the possibility of your joining them for their final round of fact-finding and due diligence, or whether they would rather go it alone. We can imagine a few basic scenarios here that may be relevant.

In one scenario, you as a parent don't have the luxury of taking time off from work and family, or purchasing a train or plane ticket to accompany your child. In such a situation you'll have to manage your child's expectations, although if it's strictly a matter of cost, some institutions may well assist you with travel as well. If you can't make the trip, there are multiple ways in which you can be involved and get your own questions answered. Start by looking with your child at the admitted students' web page, which is likely accessible through the same portal they used throughout the application process. It may contain FAQs, webinars, and contact information for parent resources.

In another scenario, your child may feel strongly about embarking alone on this leg of the journey. While it might initially be concerning, consider it as preparation for the ultimate separation and transition that awaits both of you. Ask yourself whether you are open to their doing so, and to the extent you have concerns whether they can be addressed. This may be the first time that your child has traveled on their own, and you may have basic safety worries, which you should discuss with them.

There is, finally, the possibility that the planets align and that your child wishes you to accompany them on these trips, and that you have the time and resources to do so. In such cases there will not only be events and activities for your child, but for you as a parent as well. Before embarking on such trips together, review with your child the grid on which they have arrayed their choices and the factors that will inform them, and make a game plan for how each of you will set about getting the information that you need. You might also want to have a conversation about which activities you will do together and those you will want to pursue independently. Not only will your child need their own space, particularly as they meet their potential future classmates, but you can both cover more ground by dividing and conquering. There will likely be times when the schools intentionally separate you, which will give you an opportunity to compare notes with other parents (while being careful to remember that, no matter how much you may like or relate to them, it is your child going to college, not you).

You'll also want to consider how to incorporate the views of your spouse, partner, or other adults involved in planning trips, as well as the roles you each might play. You might also want to consult your child's college counselor for their perspective.

Regardless of whether you're making college trips or not, you are very much a part of this final phase of the College Conversation, and we want to underscore one particular line of inquiry that you are likely far more suited than your child to pursue. Whether in person or virtually, you might take on the responsibility of asking questions related to the **support services** that would be available to your child at each of the institutions they are considering attending. By "support services" we mean tutoring, academic support and mentoring, health and wellness, and public safety. These can be areas of real differentiation between and among institutions. While you may have asked some of these questions throughout the search process, they will now take on new urgency and immediacy. Your queries, and additional ones posed by your child, in these areas will further inform your sense of a campus's culture and community—and the degree to which it will support your child's growth and development.

In particular we want to single out the importance of an institution's mental health supports. Numerous national studies have shown that college and university students' mental health concerns have soared in recent years. Whether or not your child will need to seek out counseling or other mental health services, you should know in advance the degree to which the institution places a priority on them. These include protocols for making appointments and average wait times to access such services, and whether those services are offered under a standard fee as part of the cost of attendance or are covered by your own health insurance or health insurance offered by the institution.

Another line of inquiry concerns the services that are offered to support your child's academic success. Many institutions have a resource center devoted to instilling in students habits and other strategies that can ensure they are able to take maximum advantage of the school's educational opportunities. These might be as basic as time management but can extend to university writing and tutoring in specific disciplines. Even if, at this point, you and your child can't imagine that they would need such assistance, remember that college is different from high school in many ways—including the amount of freedom they will have to manage their time—and you and they may find it comforting to know that this safety net exists.

In terms of assessing campus safety, one source of information that schools are federally mandated to make available, under the Clery Act, is statistics on campus crime. The easiest way to find this data may be by using the search function on the college or university's website, using "Clery Act" as the keyword. Put those figures in the context of the size of the student body and the community as a whole, and consider, too, the extent to which the institution may be focused on educating students about alcohol abuse and sexual assault. If you have follow-up questions, reach out to the school's division of public safety or the office of the dean of students.

As they visit campus, or return for follow-up visits, encourage your child to be almost journalistic in their approach. Good journalists ask pointed questions of a range of sources—in this case, students, faculty, administrators, and alumni (especially recent alumni)—and also use their powers of observation. Potential enrollees should allow themselves the time to look around, and to do so with an open mind and a critical eye.

A potential question to a current student might be, How, and under what circumstances, do students interact and engage with faculty members? Is it merely during designated office hours? Or are there other formal, or informal, ways of doing so—such as in residential settings or through take-a-professor-to-lunch programs, which many institutions underwrite? Similarly, a child might ask whether research opportunities—such as working in a faculty member's lab or doing fieldwork in the local community—are open to undergraduates, how readily available such experiences are, and how one goes about finding them. What about studying abroad, or internships, paid or otherwise?

Your child might likewise ask current students how they spend their time on the weekends, the spaces on campus where they get their work done, and the degree to which undergraduates are collaborative and supportive (as opposed to competitive). Are there short breaks in the school calendar during which some students go home but others remain on campus? Do the residence and dining halls remain open during these periods? On the financial side, did students incur any expenses that they didn't anticipate, such as specific course fees or supplies? For those students who work on campus, including through work-study—a federally supported student work program—what impact does that work have on their overall schedule?

In his role as a dean of admissions, Eric often asked first-year students early in the university's academic year what surprised them about themselves, as well as what surprised them most about the school. Your child might find it valuable to ask similar questions.

As they are in the process of gathering information, your child should avoid feeling pressured to make a decision on the spot and in that moment. Encourage them to do their fact-finding, with the understanding that distance and a period of contemplation will benefit their decision-making further down the road.

Your child may also be tempted to look for a defining moment of clarity—almost like rays of light that emerge from a cloudy sky—that is unlikely to materialize. Manage their expectations by giving them a bit of a reality check. While they may have spent years imagining where they might go off to college, and the ways it might fundamentally alter their lives, no experience in life can be perfect.

Once they've returned home, caught up on their rest, and gained a little perspective, it will be time to move the decision-making phase of the College Conversation to its conclusion. But before we do that, a brief word about a few remaining factors to consider—beginning with finances.

(E.) Factoring Financial Aid into the Final Decision

Around the time that your child received an offer of admission, they may have also been sent a **financial aid package**. Its components may have included need-based financial aid, in the form of scholarships or grants (money you will not be responsible for paying back); a job on campus—the work-study employment we referred to earlier—where students typically work between ten and twelve hours a week, and no more than twenty, per federal law; and loans, whether from the federal or state governments, or from the school itself. These will have to be paid back, typically beginning immediately after graduation.

If the college has a policy of providing merit aid pegged to academic performance or other talents, including athletic, this would also be indicated. Some parents may be surprised to learn that their child has been offered a merit scholarship for which they did not even apply. This may be an incentive offered by an institution to try to enroll those students whom they most aspire to enroll—students who, it believes, may have offers from colleges considered to be competitors. Now it is the colleges trying to lock in the students in their top quartile—with that top defined by test scores, grades, and other achievements.

So how do you, as a family, compare financial aid offers—and, if necessary, put follow-up questions to the institutions themselves, particularly if you feel the package does not sufficiently meet your family's financial expectations?

You might begin at the website of a nonprofit organization based in San Francisco called ScholarMatch. Here you can print out a document the organization calls its "Financial Aid Comparison Worksheet." You and your child can use it to make a heading for each institution and then, in the column beneath each, fill in figures in categories that include "cost of attendance" (which may be labeled "COA" in your child's financial aid letter), "grants and scholarships," and other financing options like loans and work-study. Once completed, the form should provide a handy overview to make straightforward comparisons of each school's offers. Use the worksheet as a guide for your family, perhaps in consultation with the college counselor at your high school. It can certainly inform your strategy for any follow-up.

You should feel comfortable calling a financial aid office to seek clarification or to appeal an award you feel is insufficient, perhaps due to a change in financial circumstance or any other life occurrences (such as extenuating medical bills or caring for an elderly grandparent) that you wish to bring to the attention of the college. You should not hesitate to ask for an explanation of a term or award you don't understand. In addition to your sharing additional relevant financial information, this is also an opportunity to make another point of contact on campus—specifically, an adult who can become part of your child's support network for the next four years.

Ariana Campos, the George Washington University student by way of High Tech High, stressed the importance of being persistent in any follow-up conversations with the financial aid office. She faced the challenge of getting basic financial information documents from her father, with whom she has no relationship. Because her financial aid application could not be completed, the university waived its requirements for such forms.

"Keep on calling," she recommended. "It really makes it more personal and makes someone really want to help you."

Ariana credits her mom with encouraging her not to give up in her outreach to the financial aid office. Her college counselor, Chris White, cites another factor in Ariana's strength and resilience: among her extracurricular activities is her six-days-a-week training as a Muay Thai fighter.

"It's like kickboxing, but with knees and elbows," Ariana explained, laughing as she asserted that it made her feel prepared for anything that college might throw at her.

There will also be circumstances where, informed by your worksheet, you might want one institution to clarify why its merit award was less than another's. A few cautions, though. First, need-based aid and merit aid are based on completely different criteria, so save yourself the effort of asking an institution that doesn't offer merit aid to match the award of an institution that does. Also, each institution's definition of need may be different. And so it may well be worth the phone call to ask one institution why its need-based aid award offer is less than that of another institution—and, if asked, you should feel comfortable sharing any documentation (including the actual financial aid letter from the competing institution) that supports your case for appeal. You should, however, be prepared to be told that award policies may vary between institutions.

But what about the case of two or more institutions offering your child merit aid packages of significantly different amounts? In those circumstances, you might want to make the institution with the lower award aware of the disparity, as they may be willing to make an adjustment.

As with any discussion in which large amounts of money are involved, you may find yourself at times feeling intimidated, anxious, or even upset. But be aware of the fact that the people in financial aid offices are there to help you, to the extent that they can do so under their policies, guidelines, and available resources.

One other online resource you might consider is the student loan repayment estimator on the Federal Student Aid website, sponsored by the U.S. Department of Education. Using this tool, you and your child can project how much it will take on a monthly basis to repay any loans they are considering taking out for their education.

One statistic that may be helpful: for those students who receive financial aid for their undergraduate education, the average loan debt at graduation is roughly $30,000. While interest rates and repayment terms vary, the average amount those graduates will pay back monthly is approximately $350 over a span of about ten years.

As your child approaches their final decision, they may encounter additional expenses: a **nonrefundable deposit** that confirms their intention to attend, which could range from a few hundred dollars to a few thousand. For those families who are receiving substantial financial aid, it may be possible to request a waiver for the deposit. For those who are not receiving aid, be aware that the deposit is not a supplementary charge to the full cost of attendance but instead will be subtracted from it.

Before moving on to our final activity—making the final decision—we want to be sure we very briefly address two issues that may be relevant for some readers: a waiting list decision that may still be pending, and your child's desire to consider a gap year.

(F.) If Your Child Remains on a Waiting List

After securing a spot on a waiting list, your child will find themselves in a holding pattern while still needing to move forward with other choices. We advised earlier that if a spot on the waiting list was offered and of interest, your child should notify the college as quickly as possible to ensure their consideration.

As a follow-up, there may be a specific online form that your child can use to update the institution with any additional information, such as quarterly grades or an award or accomplishment in an extracurricular activity. When such a form is offered, your child should feel confident that whatever reports they provide will be uploaded directly to their application. While your child may be tempted to send other information, such as a follow-up letter to an admissions dean, such correspondence might not make its way into the application file. Whether in the form itself or in a separate email, your child should be sure to convey the level of their ongoing interest, as the college will factor into its decision-making whether your child is likely to attend if offered a seat in the class, to the extent that openings become available for waiting list students.

The waiting list period can extend until the end of June, and most colleges will try to finalize the coming first-year class by July 1. At such time, most colleges will inform those who remain on the waiting list that it has now closed. If your child remains on a waiting list as the end of April approaches, it is imperative that they make a decision to secure a spot at an institution to which they have been admitted. If in the coming weeks they do come off a waiting list and wish to attend that institution, they can inform the previous institution that they no longer wish to attend, though any deposit they made will likely be lost.

(G.) For Those Students Considering a Gap Year

For a range of reasons, some students may decide that they wish to take a **gap year**, typically defined as a year between finishing high school and beginning college. The reasons may be cultural or religious (a Mormon mission or a year in Israel); related to military service (which is compulsory in some countries) or community service, whether locally, nationally, or abroad; or even entrepreneurial, for those students who developed a marketable idea in high school and secured funding for it. Others may have decided that they need to work for a year to help pay for their education, while still others simply feel burned out and seek a temporary change of pace.

A growing body of research indicates that students who take a gap year have higher rates of advancing from the first to second year of college, as well as progressing to graduation.

There is no shortage of information online, as well as any number of books about options for gap years. Many for-profit businesses cater to students wishing to take a gap year, as well as nonprofit organizations—including one called Global Citizen Year, which offers what it calls an "immersion-based international bridge year." Global Citizen, like other nonprofits in this area, provides scholarships—some covering the full cost of attendance, which is up to $32,500—to students who qualify based on need. In many instances your child can use the same FAFSA form that they completed for college financial aid as a means to be considered for aid to take a gap year.

If your child is interested in pursuing a gap year, they will first need to accept an offer of admission from a college or university and then ask that college, in writing, for permission to defer their enrollment for a year. The college will then ask the reason for the deferral, and how your child intends to spend the year.

(H.) Time to Choose

By this point in the College Conversation, you and your child have come off the road, with your due diligence—in-person and virtual— largely complete by mid- to late April. It is time for your child to narrow their choices and make their decision.

Some may be selecting between two or three choices; others may have more. All of those schools have earned their way onto your child's list for a reason, and each deserves full consideration. If your child has multiple choices, don't be surprised if they seem a bit overwhelmed by the decision. An article published in 2004 on the website of the American Psychological Association describes several studies suggesting that when consumers have too many options from which to choose, they can become almost paralyzed by the decision-making process. This dynamic may be further heightened when taking into account such factors as the wiring of the teenage brain—and your child's perception that this is a high-stakes decision, possibly the biggest they have had to make up to this point in their lives.

Assure your child again that there is no perfect choice here, and that, with your support, they will make the best decision they can with the information at hand. Give them, and yourself, confidence that their process thus far has been strong and that it will yield further dividends as they consider their options.

ACTIVITY #12: Narrowing the Field

For this exercise, you and your child might return to a familiar and comfortable spot in or around your home. Whether you are at your kitchen table or somewhere else where you can have a private conversation, keep things uncluttered. For your child to make the decision, you and they will likely not need much more than the final grid from Activity #11—the one with the C's along the top and the names of the colleges down the side—and the financial aid comparison worksheet.

If your child has made their grid by hand, they might want to make a photocopy; if they've used an Excel worksheet or Google Doc, it's time to "save as." We both tend to be very visual and suggest your child engage in this exercise with markers or highlighting on-screen. Consider using three markers or highlighters—one green, one yellow, and one red. While any colors will do, of course, we're seeking to make use of a traffic signal metaphor.

First, your child should do some rough differentiating and ranking within each of the categories. In the section on curriculum, for example, go beyond the basic question of whether a particular major that may be of interest is offered, and encourage your child to consider the full breadth of a college's academic offerings, including the general education requirements (including the distributive requirements mentioned earlier) and the opportunity to take elective courses. These have likely been the subject of conversations your child has been having over a period of time, including with you and their counselor. Now, gazing through the lens of an admitted student, they should try to imagine embarking on an academic journey at each institution, with the curriculum as an academic road map. How does that make them feel?

For those schools that have a clear advantage in your child's mind, they might color that category green. For those institutions whose curricular offerings don't quite measure up to the others, use yellow to indicate neutrality and red to indicate apprehension. The goal here is that their shadings in particular categories will make it easier for your child to weigh their options—and to ultimately decide which variables in a college they value over others, and which become determinative in their decision. Earlier in the book we suggested that you share with your child the process you embarked on to choose a first home or apartment to rent or buy, when you had to consider such factors as proximity to public transportation, school district, price, square footage, and neighbors. This same process can be useful for them now.

For cost, you and your child should be sure to reference some of the figures on the financial aid comparison worksheet—and, to the extent some schools require loans or out-of-pocket expenses, the feasibility for your family to meet those financial demands.

We hope that you have already had conversations with your child about the degree to which finances will be a factor in their decision, so this shouldn't be new. As a final choice looms, do be aware of your emotions, and theirs, around cost—and ensure you are talking openly about the feelings you each may be experiencing.

Depending on your child, and your family dynamic, they might do this exercise separately or together with you. You might also each do your own version of the exercise. If the latter is the case, do be careful to take into consideration the impact that your differentiations and rankings might have on their own choices. Give them the latitude, ownership, and independence to make a decision, which will serve them well as they head into the transition to college and life. But because you also are their parent, and have an adult perspective and life experience that deserves consideration, try to find an appropriate balance between your own perspective and your child's that works within the dynamics of your family.

If there is another parent, partner, or spouse involved in this final decision, be conscious of the potential effect that their opinion may have on your child's decision—and whether those views conflict with, or are consistent with, your child's and your own. To the extent that you and that other adult have conflicting views on narrowing the college choice, your child might find those differing views to be either helpful or confusing. Similarly, if you and that other adult are in agreement, don't let your consensus crowd out your child's views.

Your child may wish to tackle this exercise in a single sitting, or to consider each column with time for breaks between—perhaps even overnight, if time permits. Set aside whatever time it takes for them to maintain a sense of calm (though we know that is a relative term) and clearheadedness. If things get heated, or your child feels overwhelmed, encourage them to pause, and explain to them that high stress or anxiety can be an impediment to clear decision-making. Whether it takes them a few hours or several days, they might try to color in every box in their grid, in order for the clearest possible picture to emerge. As you both look horizontally across the line for each college, your child might first note the schools where the red shading is heavy. Now is the time to take those colleges off the list. As they then turn to those schools dotted with yellows and greens, you might guide them a bit on how to calibrate those factors that ultimately matter most to them. For some students, this may be a matter of simply tallying those colleges that scored the highest number of green lights. Others may need to ask themselves whether one school's green in the category of curriculum outweighs another's in the box for community. At a certain point, perhaps after one last check-in with their college counselor, the time will come to make a decision.

As noted, many colleges and universities still have a deadline of May 1 at 11:59 p.m. in the time zone where your child resides or where the college is located. This is known as the **candidate reply date**, which is when your child is expected to convey their intention to enroll at the college they have chosen, as well as to decline the other colleges that have offered them admission.

We strongly advise that, if possible, your child not wait until the final hour of the final day to make their decision and communicate it. We have several reasons for this recommendation.

The first is technical in nature: systems can easily become overloaded and crash, and your internet connection can go down. Meanwhile, your child will likely be facing other time pressures, as their lives as high school students—extracurricular and academic—still go on. Remember that if your child is taking Advanced Placement courses, those tests are typically offered in the first two weeks of May, so they are preparing for them (ideally) in the last week of April.

Take special notice when May 1 or any other reply deadline falls on a weekend—when admissions offices, to say nothing of their high school college counseling office, are most likely closed. In such circumstances, there may not be anyone readily available to answer last-minute questions.

Finally, consider the emotional risks of making a final decision, and racing to communicate it to a college, in the last few minutes before a deadline—particularly in the middle of the night, when no one is at their clearest or best. A frantic choice made under those conditions could result not only in a sleepless night but pangs of regret the next morning.

While your child, and you, may need as much time as possible in the final week before a decision is due, block out a cushion period in which they can make that decision and let it sit for a while before they press the notification button. In that interim they can imagine they have made their choice and quite literally visualize themselves as a student at that college or university come fall.

And then the moment will come to push that button.

We hope that when they make the final determination of where they will enroll in college, they will do so filled with feelings of promise and possibility about this next and exciting stage of their lives, and with the confidence and conviction that their decision-making process was sound.

(I.) The Moments Immediately After the Decision

At this point some celebration is in order—for them, and you—as well as some space for much-needed rest. Again, encourage your child to resist the temptation to immediately go on social media with an announcement or proclamation of the decision they've just made. Even in our fast-paced, let-it-all-rip-online world—or perhaps as an antidote to it—your child might want to let that decision be their own, if even for just a short period of time.

Don't be surprised if your child expresses, yet again, some feelings of letdown or anticlimax. As a society we too often build up the college process to a level of stratospheric expectation that may not align with reality. It is important to let your child know that such emotions are normal. Their feelings at this time may also include some second-guessing. This is another point where your insight into your child, and how they make and process decisions, will be critical. Second-guessing is, of course, not unusual, especially when someone is presented with an array of compelling choices, and overcoming it requires some projecting into the future with a leap of faith.

Here again, reassure them that their process was careful and well-thought-out, that there are no perfect decisions, and that they made the best choice possible given the information at hand and the time allowed.

In some rare cases that second-guessing may not abate but may intensify to the point of causing anxiety and deep regret about a choice. If that's the case, and depending on your relationship with your child, you will want to ask them some pointed, even probing, questions.

If the feeling of regret pertains to lingering disappointment about not being admitted to one of those schools that they considered aspirational, your role will entail helping them to reach a point of acceptance, at least for their first year. If those feelings extend deep into the first year, we'll have some advice in the next section of *The College Conversation* about the transfer process. You might remind them that they will bear responsibility for embracing the opportunities that await them, and to prepare over the coming months to make the most of that experience.

But what about the rare case of a child who chose one school over another but remains convinced that they made the wrong choice? You will have to try to determine whether their anxiety is rooted in the choice itself, or perhaps in an overall wariness about going off to college at all, regardless of which school it is. You might even want to bring your child's college counselor back into the conversation to help address any lingering questions and, we hope, allay any remaining concerns.

We'll have much more to say about the transition process, and its various emotions, in the next and final section of *The College Conversation.*

PART V

*Conversations About
the Transition*

W e're not done just yet.

While so much of the college process seems pointed like a GPS toward the moment when your child confirms where they will be going to school, finally reaching that milestone unlocks a series of new, time-sensitive decisions that they will have to make over a relatively short period. This phase begins with the six weeks or so (depending on your child's school calendar) between the deposit they made confirming their college enrollment through the moment they will stride across the stage with their high school diploma in hand.

We're committed in the final pages of this book to support you, as you support your child, not only through the transition from high school to college but on from there through the end of their first year. We also want to provide insight for you as you transition from being the parent of a high school senior to that of a college student— amid all the emotions you will be feeling, whether it's your oldest child you are sending off or your youngest.

As you're about to discover, your child has an extraordinary number of tasks to execute and choices to make in a compressed period that will shape the arc of their first year of college. Among our goals here is to highlight a number of those decisions, so you will know what to expect, as well as to provide you with prompts for engaging in conversations in which you might serve as a sounding board and partner in brainstorming, as well as a lever of accountability, including around some important deadlines.

We also want to buttress you in your role as a support to your child during those critical first few weeks when they are adjusting to campus—subject to a revised set of rules of the road and guardrails you will want to agree upon (including around your respective expectations for communication during this period). And since incoming students can't ultimately "know until they go," we'll have particular advice for parents or other adults whose child may arrive home for the December holidays and announce that they wish to transfer.

(A.) On the Importance of Your Child's Finishing High School Strong

We've all been drivers on long car rides when, as the ultimate destination comes into view, we're tempted to take our eyes off the road or foot off the gas, particularly as a result of fatigue. With the decision phase of the College Conversation now behind them, your child may be experiencing moments much like this. But you need to not only help them keep their focus during these final weeks of high school but also encourage them to engage in a series of culminating academic, extracurricular, and community experiences, with the hope, of course, that these events come off as planned. After so many months of waiting and anticipation, they should now be able to pause to take a breath and be present for these special moments. As an adult, you're well aware that there are rarely respites like this in life.

It's easy to understand the temptation they may feel to ease up on studying for final exams or completing remaining projects or papers. But in addition to staying true to any lofty ideals, there are very practical and serious reasons why they need to finish their high school career in a position of strength. You may or may not be aware that when your child committed to enroll at the college they will attend, they likely signed an agreement in which they acknowledged that their admission was contingent upon certain expectations being met during the balance of their senior year. This enrollment contract includes a provision that they remain in good standing academically and a responsible citizen of their school and community. At various points in *The College Conversation*, we have cited ways that students could jeopardize their acceptance status—particularly in an age of social media, when an ill-advised comment they intended to be kept private suddenly becomes exposed and shared with a college admissions office. In his role as a dean of admissions, Eric has experienced firsthand how a parent disappointed in their child's own admission outcome might turn vindictive, to the point of sharing damaging information about another child with the intention of getting their offer of admission rescinded.

We believe this enrollment agreement is so important that we advise you to sit down with your child and have them read it aloud to you. By doing so, they not only acknowledge their responsibility for upholding the agreement but their personal commitment to be held accountable for doing so. The last document that a college counselor will upload through an admissions portal is a student's final transcript, with end-of-senior-year grades and confirmation of graduation. Those students whose grades have dipped precipitously, or who have failed to graduate for any reason, will likely receive a letter from the admissions office asking for a written explanation of the circumstances. The admissions office seeks this supplemental information to gain insight into what may be happening below the surface—such as a family emergency—and to make sure your child is in the best position to succeed. In those cases where there is no good reason for a sudden academic free fall, an accepted student may well be informed that their admission status is at risk. Such instances are not uncommon: Eric estimates that each year during his tenure as dean he sent a warning letter to several dozen of the 2,400 or so students enrolling in the first-year class.

(B.) Decisions and Actions Between Your Child's High School Graduation and Their Arrival at College

After the admissions office has completed all its decisions and the entering class members have committed to enroll, various other offices on campus, including those that manage academics, housing, dining, finance, student life, and health and wellness, enter the picture. Each may well reach out to incoming students directly, with tasks to complete and choices to be made. It's a lot to keep track of, which means your child is going to need your support. We'll now briefly walk you through what will become an extended to-do list, followed by prompts to help you and your child establish your roles and responsibilities at this stage of the College Conversation. Every college or university will have its own version of this list, with tasks and deadlines arrayed in a particular sequence and a vocabulary specific to the culture (and branding) of that institution. In assembling our description of such a list on the following pages, we were informed by, among other sources, a framework known as the Penn10, a checklist of ten action items provided to every first-year and transfer student at the University of Pennsylvania. Regardless of the particulars issued by your child's school, we believe that the items that follow will help you to guide your child in executing the necessary tasks:

- **Set up a student identification and portal**
  This will become your child's gateway for the many actions to follow, including registering for a student ID card and, perhaps, setting up a school email account, as well as serving as a hub for communication and the bundling of an array of services and information, including choosing a dining plan.

- **Join Facebook and other social media groups (official and unofficial) for admitted students**
  Your child may already be active in these communities, having joined within minutes of their admission notification. If not, they should take part in at least a few of these groups, some of which will serve as a forum for communication and community throughout the college experience and beyond. Remind your child that anything they post in these forums will be broadcast to an audience of classmates and university administrators, and reinforce the need for them to exercise good judgment.

- **Apply for housing and choose a roommate**
  Colleges vary in their approach to on-campus housing registration, with some permitting an immediate sign-up upon a commitment to enroll, and others waiting until an established date on the calendar. In terms of selecting a roommate, your child may be presented with at least one of the following options: a request to fill out a survey indicating various lifestyle habits, such as whether they are early or late to bed, tidy or sloppy, followed by a matching process; an entirely random

assignment, which some studies have shown to be surprisingly effective in preparing students to live compatibly with others; or an invitation to request a specific roommate, whom they may know from high school or have just met through admitted student days or in a class social media group.

- **Arrange to pay the first semester (or trimester) tuition and other expenses, and ensure any financial aid is applied**
The initial tuition bill may arrive on or around July 1, with payment due at some point prior to the first day of classes. Indeed, your child may not be able to register for classes if at least a portion of the bill has not been paid. If you prefer to spread out payments, you may be able to do so in installments, as arranged through the institution or a third-party provider, with a fee charged. You or your child should ensure that whatever financial aid is being provided by the institution, as well as aid from any outside scholarships, has been applied to their account, including, where applicable, provisions for a work-study job on campus. There can sometimes be a lag in the posting of scholarships and other aid, so you and your child should pay attention—and stay in close communication with the office on campus responsible for billing. There will likely be an opportunity for you to establish your own login as an authorized user of your child's billing account, which will enable you to make payments and monitor credits. Finally, you may be presented with an opportunity, prior to the start of classes, to purchase **tuition insurance**, likely from an outside vendor. Such policies can offer peace of mind and ensure that if your child has to withdraw at any point in the academic year, including for health reasons, you'll be able to recover at least a portion of your financial expenditures, including, perhaps, tuition and housing fees paid in advance. Some colleges, even in cases where tuition insurance has not been purchased, may permit

a student to withdraw in the first couple of weeks of a semester with little to no financial penalty.

- **Update required immunizations and establish health insurance**

  Your child will likely be unable to register for classes without providing proof of a range of immunizations. Some schools may require submission of these and other health records, including a recent physical exam, months in advance of the first day of school, so be sure to plan ahead in making the necessary appointments. Your child will also be asked whether they wish to purchase health insurance directly from the college or university, or to opt out if they remain on your family's health plan.

- **Familiarize themselves with the college's health and wellness and other support services**

  Long before your child arrives on campus, you and they should explore the various support services made available by the college or university in areas that may include physical fitness, mental health, social life, financial literacy, spiritual life, and academics. Your child may need to satisfy requirements in some of these areas prior to the start of classes, such as completion of short online courses, including those intended to promote healthy relationships and to prevent sexual assault and substance abuse.

- **Make contact with an academic adviser in preparation for registering for first-term courses**

  Your child will be assigned an academic adviser, perhaps as early as the summer, who will serve as a resource and point person as they get up to speed on academic requirements and begin to explore the university's course offerings. Deadlines for the actual selection of courses can vary, with some institutions permitting students to make preliminary choices prior to arrival followed by a sampling or shopping period during the first few weeks of classes, in which course selections can be modified. This might be a good time for you and your child to look together at the institution's academic calendar to determine how long they have to lock in their choices. In addition, most colleges have firm deadlines for when your child may drop a course in which they have registered without the course and grade appearing on their transcript. Failure to meet those deadlines could result in your child receiving an official notification, again on the transcript, of having withdrawn from a particular course—or perhaps even a failing grade that could weigh down their grade point average. You and your child, perhaps in consultation with their academic adviser, should also be aware of policies (likely with strict deadlines) that may permit some courses to be taken on a pass-fail basis, meaning they will not receive a letter grade in the course, easing their transition into college academics.

- **Register to participate in orientation activities, and engage in and complete any academic work assigned in advance of their arrival**
  Throughout the lead-in to your child's first day of classes, they will be offered an opportunity to sign up for a variety of orientation activities. Some will take place on campus, in the days just before the start of the first term, and encompass areas like academics (including placement exams, such as in math or a foreign language); icebreakers, where they can get to know other students (including in their residence hall); resource fairs (including the range of support services referenced above); and an introduction to campus traditions, including the teaching of the school fight song or reviewing highlights from the college's history. There may be an academic activity centered on a common theme—as well as

an assignment for everyone to read the same book, to be discussed in groups large or small. There may also be a culminating social event, whether on campus or at a historical or cultural site in the surrounding community. Your child should also be on the lookout for pre-orientation activities— some of which may take place prior to the official move-in date—which could range from several days spent in small groups in the outdoors or devoted to a community service project. Other pre-orientation programs, which may be by invitation, are intended to help ensure that students are ready for the transition from high school to college academic work. Finally, you as a parent should be on the lookout for orientation activities geared specifically to you—including those that will take place on campus after you have dropped off your child but before you say goodbye.

- **Explore the availability of potential accommodations (learning and physical)**
  Your child's middle school or high school may have provided them with certain academic accommodations related to learning differences. They may have been granted extended time for tests, or the option to take a test using a keyboard instead of writing by hand. Others may have required enhanced audio or visual aids, such as a textbook in large print or read aloud. To the extent that you or your child wishes to pursue similar supports in college, we encourage you to plan ahead—including making contact with the appropriate office, which may have a name like the Learning Resource Center, even before arriving on campus. In some instances, your child may be required to provide supporting documentation, including an updated evaluation from a specialist. Your child may also have physical requirements that are relevant to their housing—such as the need for a first-floor room, to address mobility issues, or a room without carpeting, to alleviate

respiratory allergies, such as to dust and mold. Here again communication with the college in advance is key.

As you work your way through these and other checklists, revisit—and likely revise—the ground rules and boundaries you established with your child early in the College Conversation. You should consider setting clear parameters together, identifying which of you is responsible for completing—and thus owning—the various tasks and forms referenced above. Going forward you might also introduce the idea that as they make the transition from living under your roof, their responsibilities will only grow—and that with their newfound independence you will be taking a lesser role in helping them manage their daily lives. There will be no shortage of emotions associated with this transition process—for your child as well as for you—so be open with each other about what you may be feeling.

(c.) Conversations About Laying a Foundation for Success

As your child prepares for college, engage them in conversation about laying a foundation for a successful experience there, particularly in their first year. A nonprofit organization called Complete College America even has a label for this critically important period, which they call the Momentum Year. Studies have shown that students who succeed in advancing from the first to second year of college are more likely to go on to complete their education and earn a degree, particularly within the preferred four years or even over the course of as many as six years, which has become the time frame against which national benchmarks are set.

While your child's earning a degree may be your ultimate measure of higher-education success, we hope you'll also discuss with them how you each define that success—whether it's grades earned; academic honors; leadership roles and job placement; or outcomes that are harder to measure, like fostering lifelong friendships, igniting a long-term curiosity about a particular subject, or the very act of learning itself.

Regardless of your definition, a review of research ranging from sources as varied as the American Association of Colleges and Universities to Gallup, as well as any number of physicians, psychologists, and psychiatrists, provides insight into a half dozen or so behaviors, attitudes, and actions that correlate with student success in that first year.

To help you help your child, let's examine some of those building blocks.

Advocacy and Outreach

A defining factor in students' success in college is the degree to which they seek out professors as well as peers to establish the relationships that can make them feel part of the fabric of the institution. While these individuals can never replace you, they do become part of a larger support circle.

One such person may be an individual they have already met: an admissions officer who visited their high school, or whom they encountered during a campus visit—as well as, perhaps, a professor whose class they sat in on. Even a vaguely familiar face can be the equivalent of a lighthouse beacon across the expanse of an unfamiliar campus, guiding your child's way at this early stage of their journey. More formally, their academic adviser will perform these and other functions, as will faculty who may be assigned to their residence halls. They will also be introduced to older students who have been trained as advisers within the residence halls, including those with the title **residence adviser**, or **RA**.

Among the most important pieces of advice you might give your child is to feel comfortable and confident about reaching out to the professors teaching their courses. In the **syllabus** your child will receive on the first day of class—a document that will outline expectations for the course, including assignments and exams—the professor will likely list their office hours. These are periods in which professors make themselves available not only to answer questions about the classwork but also to get to know your child. Research by Gallup in partnership with Strada Education Network found that students who sought out professors were more likely to feel a sense of belonging on campus. By engaging with their teachers in academic settings outside of class, students also reported feeling that they were being taught by an individual who "cares about me as a person" and "makes me excited about learning."

You might also suggest to your child that they keep an eye out for formal programming intended to foster the connections between students and faculty, such as those that pay for a student or group of students to have lunch with a professor. There may also be weekly events within academic departments, such as an informal talk, with free food provided as an added enticement.

While it may require encouragement on your part, especially for a child who is reticent or introverted, our advice is that they put themselves out there. Though they may feel uncomfortable at first, these are opportunities for your child to have a valuable and enriching set of conversations early in their college year.

We want to end this section with a plug for an area of campus that is often overlooked—particularly in our digital age: the college library. For those parents who attended college themselves, your enduring memory of the library may be of being shushed into silence by a librarian or sequestering yourself deep in the stacks to write a research paper.

You may be surprised to learn that many campus libraries have been re-envisioned as dynamic spaces—often with on-site cafés—that encourage collaborative work. In the era of Google, the modern-day librarian is there to help your child organize and synthesize what may seem like the overwhelming amount of information available to them. There may also be smaller satellite libraries dotting the campus presided over by librarians who specialize in fields ranging from the fine arts to biomedical sciences.

Time Management and Executive Function

From kindergarten to the twelfth grade, your child's school day was highly structured and regimented, as was, in all likelihood, their after-school time. With their transition to college, they may be in class for as few as a dozen hours a week—leaving them huge blocks of unscheduled time that they are responsible for programing.

This is time that they will devote to homework and other academic assignments, as well as activities and perhaps a part-time job, to say nothing of meals and socializing with friends. Some students will be able to adapt the time management skills that made them successful in high school to now fit the task at hand in college, whether it involves dividing up a two-hundred-page reading assignment across five days or populating their calendars with due dates for research papers, and then working backward to establish interim targets.

But others will need to seek out resources to learn these skills. These involve not only time management, such as combating procrastination, but also executive functions, such as organizing and prioritizing multiple projects. To the extent you believe your child might benefit from support systems like these, which are widely available on college and university campuses, you might recommend that they be proactive and do so before they fall behind. Present these opportunities to them not as remedying deficiencies but as strategies that can help them meet their goals, maximize how much they learn, and minimize stress.

Forming an Identity and Finding Community Outside the Classroom

So much of what your child will remember long after they have graduated from college are those experiences that took place outside the walls of their classrooms. Some of them might be extensions of pursuits from high school—which can have the added benefit of providing familiarity at a time in their lives when everything and everyone seems so new. Other activities might offer both the excitement of novelty and the prospect of a fresh start. One welcome difference from high school is that your child need no longer engage in activities out of a sense that they need to fill in all the lines provided on a college application.

One way to survey the range of student organizations available on campus is during an activity fair, which will likely be held during the first few weeks of classes. At the very least, encourage your child to get involved in something with the modest objective of becoming engaged in an outside pursuit to counterbalance what may be a fairly intense academic experience. Here again, Gallup found in a survey of college students that those who felt successful were "active in extracurricular activities and organizations." These could also enable them to widen their circle of friends beyond their classes and residence halls, and even counteract early pangs of homesickness by offering them opportunities to have shared and meaningful experiences with their classmates.

While we generally don't advise that students seek out formal internships as they're settling in during their first semester or even first year, we do want them to give thought early on to how they can connect their classroom work to hands-on experiences across campus and within the surrounding community. A student studying political science and government could contact a faculty member who does opinion polling; a nursing student could volunteer their time at a local clinic; a student interested in education could tutor children at an elementary school. Another insight from Gallup and its survey of college students who considered themselves successful: many engaged in projects outside the classroom that extended over the course of multiple terms.

Sleep, Nutrition, and Exercise

This is one of those areas where common sense aligns with research: students who pay attention to their sleep (seven to nine hours most nights) as well as eating a balanced diet and exercising (thirty minutes most days) tend to not only be successful in college but also lead healthier lifestyles.

Because this advice is far easier given than done, urge your child to take advantage of campus resources that can guide them into proper habits, whether it's exercise classes offered at the on-campus fitness center, consultations with a nutritionist who may be posted in the dining halls or health center, or campus-wide talks on good sleep hygiene.

Stress, Anxiety, and Depression

A recent study published by the American Psychological Association estimated that worldwide, roughly one out of every three first-year college students experiences symptoms consistent with a mental health disorder—including anxiety, panic attacks, or depression. Parents need to be especially attuned to any signs that their child might be struggling.

While these findings are obviously a source of great concern, the stigma associated with mental illness on campus has largely been lifted, as evidenced by campus-wide dialogue and the broad availability of support services, including professional counseling, peer-to-peer training, and resources to learn strategies for combating and managing stress and anxiety.

For those parents who would like to gain a deeper understanding of the mental health challenges faced by college students today, we recommend a book we referenced earlier, *The Stressed Years of Their Lives: Helping Your Kid Survive and Thrive During Their College Years*. The authors—B. Janet Hibbs, a psychologist and family therapist, and Anthony Rostain, a professor of psychiatry and pediatrics—provide practical advice and information for students and parents, including behavioral warning signs, strategies for better mental health, and, where warranted, questions to ask about potential treatment and other services.

Managing a Student Budget and a Part-Time Job

In all likelihood your child will be balancing the hours devoted to a part-time job with all the other time demands of their college experience. As you discuss how they will fit work into their schedule, you may wish to revisit their financial aid package, which may include references to a job under the Federal Work-Study Program that could require ten to twenty hours of their time per week and in which they can earn up to four thousand dollars per year.

While the phrase "work-study" may be something of a misnomer—

we prefer "study-work," because they are students first—the places on campus where they will be working (whether it's the admissions office, a dining hall, or a library) will likely take into account the academic demands on them. But the key is for your child to identify early on the times they need to be in class—as well as the dates of big exams and deadlines for research papers—and then share those with their employers.

Students who are employed part-time but not in a work-study capacity, whether on campus or off, have to be realistic about the hours they can devote to a job, balanced, of course, against the money they need to earn to help pay for their education. In a bit of a vicious cycle, studies have shown that too many hours spent working while in college can be a factor in students' dropping out. Research by College Track, a community-based organization committed to students' success, found that a job commitment of more than fifteen hours per week had a negative impact on students' grade point averages.

Once your child has been at school for a month or so, you'll both have a better sense of what constitutes a realistic monthly budget. They will have a better handle on overhead costs, like books, which will be useful information as they and you plan budgets for future semesters. They will also gain insight into how they are using their campus meal plan, and the extent to which they are spending money on food beyond what they have allocated. For example, your child may have signed up for twenty-one "all you can eat" meals per week, at a fairly hefty expense, only to conclude that it's not only too much food but that the plan does not align with their hectic schedule. In such a situation, the college dining services may allow some adjustments, with dedicated meal plans replaced by more flexible spending options.

This could lead to a broader conversation about spending that is truly discretionary—including for such items as late-night pizza, movies, and other entertainment—and steps you might take together to establish, manage, and, where necessary, adjust that budget.

The Role of Struggling and Failure in Success

For children who have known nothing but straight A's in high school, the first semester of college may be something of a wake-up call for them—and you—especially when they receive what may be their first B-minus, or worse. It's not unusual for students accustomed to being at the top of their class to have the unfamiliar experience of finding themselves suddenly feeling average when surrounded by many other students who were perched at the summit of their own high schools.

Hard as it might be to convey, encourage your child to embrace and learn from these academic challenges and setbacks. Assure them that by doing so, they will grow—a message that they may well greet with skepticism. Urge them to respond to their frustration or disappointment not by being hard on themselves but by engaging in some of the actions and behaviors we outline above—perhaps, chief among them, seeking out their professors and utilizing other academic supports.

In struggling academically or otherwise, your child may convey to you a feeling that they don't belong at the college or university where they have enrolled. Researchers have found this to be particularly acute for young people who are in the first generation of their family to attend college, or from other backgrounds historically underrepresented in American higher education. **Imposter syndrome** is a name that has been adapted from a term coined in the late 1970s—imposter phenomenon—in a study describing high-achieving women who nonetheless felt a sense of "self-perceived intellectual phoniness and fraud." These feelings can lead to anxiety, stress, and depression.

To the extent that your child may share with you feelings like these, Eric has some pointed advice for you and them: if the admissions committee determined that your child merited a place on their campus, then they belong there and are more than capable of doing the work. And it's not just that they deserve to be there: that same admissions committee believed that your child had something to contribute to that campus community. These assurances aren't intended to dismiss your child's feelings. If relaying Eric's counsel doesn't provide some comfort, then they might avail themselves of some of the resources outlined in this section.

D. Drop-off, Departure, and Check-in Points Thereafter

Much of this section will be devoted to providing advice to parents whose children will be residing on campus. But first we want to say just a brief word to those whose children will be commuting to college from home.

Please be aware that the rhythms of your child's new schedule will be so radically different from those in high school that you'll feel as if a stranger or tenant with erratic hours has just moved into your home. Understand that they may need to be in the library until ten at night to finish a paper, or are sleeping in because their first class is not until noon. Like their counterparts on campus, they, too, are going through significant adjustments to college life. In light of their class times, assignments, and exams, perhaps coupled with a part-time job, it may be unrealistic for you to expect them to eat dinner with you as they always did or take care of a younger sibling; indeed, these responsibilities could become a barrier to their doing their best in school.

For those of you who may be about to experience your first college drop-off, or perhaps your second or even third, recognize that every child (and parent) is different. We'll leave it to you and your child to navigate, together, the various feelings you may each have about separating and letting go. We do, however, want to suggest that you take a moment with them to establish some ground rules regarding your respective expectations for how you will communicate with each other in the coming days, weeks, and months. These shouldn't be completely new but instead represent another revision of the guardrails and boundaries you established early in the College Conversation.

If you are a parent of a certain age who attended college, your means of communicating with those back home may have consisted of a pay phone at the end of your dorm room hallway that charged by the minute (with long distance at a premium), at least for those who didn't call collect. Fast-forward to today, where data plans are unlimited and you and your child can be in contact with each other instantaneously via cell, text, FaceTime, Facebook, WhatsApp, Instagram, and any number of virtual platforms.

Our strong advice is that you each give thought to how—and how often—you want to be in touch during this time of transition. Again, we defer to you and your child to establish the parameters that are most appropriate for you both. But among the questions you might want to pose to your child, as well as to a partner and perhaps yourself, is where you want to draw the line between making yourself accessible and allowing them the time and space to work things through independently, as well as by drawing on the support services and other resources around them.

Given the ready availability of technology, you really can provide 24/7 "customer service," if you choose. We believe that you should not. Of course there will be some moments of urgency, perhaps conveyed by text, when an immediate response is indeed warranted. But at other times consider the virtues of a bit of restraint, which could also help foster self-reliance. Moreover, you may have a deadline you are trying to meet at work, or another child to whom you need to attend, and might not be in a position to respond immediately.

What about those times where it is you reaching out, wanting an update or a sense of how your child is doing? We believe these touch points are extremely important in the early days and weeks of their transition, because as the adult in their lives who knows them best, you'll be particularly attuned to shifts in their mood or any escalation in their anxiety. You might use the headings in the previous section as a frame for conversations with your child during this period. These prompts could bring to light challenges they may be facing, giving you an opportunity to strategize with them. What's important is that you set times at which you might check in, and other times when you probably shouldn't (such as first thing on a Saturday morning) and the frequency of contact.

One role you may also be asked to play is that of a sounding board. Your child may want to discuss classes they are interested in taking, activities on which they are considering embarking, and concerns about whether there are enough hours in the day for them to do all that they want to accomplish. Your most valuable contribution might be simply to listen, at least initially, and to reassure them that they are capable of making decisions like these on their own. Where you are inclined to give advice, be mindful of the impact of what you say and the weight it may carry.

There may be opportunities in the fall, such as during a family weekend if there is one, for you to check in with your child. Depending on how far your child's college is from home, as well as your other responsibilities, making such a trip might not be possible. But if you can do so, events like these can provide a follow-up to the orientation that you and your child may have participated in earlier in the semester. These are also opportunities for you to touch base more thoroughly. Be on the lookout for openings where you might invite your child's friends to join you—subject, of course, to whether that is something your child encourages—especially in those instances where a roommate's parents may not have been able to attend an organized weekend on campus. An added bonus may be that you will gain additional perspective on what it is like to be a student at the college.

Thanksgiving break can also be a moment to touch base—again, depending on distance and resources, since it may not be possible for your child to come home then, particularly in cases where classes resume the following Monday morning. If your child does come home for this holiday—which can be as long as three months after you dropped them off and perhaps last saw them—be aware that you may observe significant changes in them. These could include new opinions (and a newfound desire to express them) as well as new sleep patterns and shifts in overall demeanor. We suggest you take it all in calmly, including their own declarations of independence, and be cautious about overreacting.

(E.) The (Potential) Transfer Conversation

As you embark on the check-ins we describe above, you may detect in your child an escalating sense that they are unhappy with their college choice—to the point that they tell you they want to make a change. In this section we'll provide guidance for parents, guardians, or others seeking to counsel a student contemplating a transfer from one four-year institution to another. As the parent of a potential transfer, you may be feeling as if you let your child down in this process. But the fact remains that they—supported by you—made the best decision they could, with the information and options available to them at the time.

In some instances, your child may have enrolled in a college that was never one of their top choices, despite their best efforts to construct a balanced list. And while having made the best of it, they would like to reapply to an institution that didn't admit them the first time around. In other cases, your child may be in college exactly where they always thought they wanted to be, yet the reality proved quite different than they expected. Or they may be responding to an invitation from another four-year college—perhaps one they applied to initially, or not—seeking to entice them to consider a switch. Transfer recruitment tactics like these—which may draw on the same databases assembled by colleges when your child was taking standardized tests, or on lists of those who turned down a college's initial offer of admission—were long off-limits. But such strategies are now permitted as a result of an agreement referenced earlier between the antitrust division of the U.S. Justice Department and the professional association for college admissions officers.

When your child raises the possibility of transferring, the first step for you as a parent is to assess what is underpinning that desire and motivation.

Like a physician ruling out various diagnoses, you will want to ask them questions intended to ferret out the reasons why they are feeling this way, and whether a transfer might indeed offer the prospect of relief.

Begin by acknowledging to yourself that children change over the eight months or more since they made their college decision. To echo our earlier observation that they can't really "know until they go," they have by now gathered quite a bit of data about themselves and the actual fit between them and their college.

As you embark on this conversation with them, consider framing it in terms of the initial index card they created in Activity #1, as well as the four basic categories of what they were seeking in a college that guided you both through Activity #10 in this book: environmental, academic, student life, and X factor. How, during their first few months of college, did these actually play out?

Let's look at a few examples of questions to pose to your child to better understand their position.

Environmental: Are there aspects of the college's environment—such as its location or size, or whether it is rural or urban—that, now that your child has experienced it, are no longer appealing? And if so, why?

Academic: Does your child feel that, academically, the other students are overly competitive about grades—or, alternately, intellectually apathetic and disengaged? For the child who thought they had a clear academic path, such as a particular major, and who chose a college largely based on that, have the courses they have taken thus far prompted a rethinking? And if they are now inclined to study a different subject, are there feasible options available at the college? Have they tried to connect with a faculty member to discuss the matter?

Student life: Have they made friends who value and appreciate them, and who have similar interests? Have they found activities that give their lives on campus a sense of joy, meaning, and engagement? Is there a pervasive culture at the school—such as around the use of alcohol and drugs—that your child believed they could navigate, but perhaps they now have doubts?

X factor: One of the key factors in your child's college decision may have been a niche particular to this institution that cut across the prior categories, such as a robust study abroad program or a vibrant off-campus arts scene. If that is no longer of interest, has the appeal of that school diminished?

For the purposes of this conversation, we're going to assume that you are having this discussion with your child during their winter break. If that's the case, then one option, of course, is to have them return to campus for the next term with an action plan. Because many institutions' transfer applications for the following fall term are not due until spring, your child may have some time in the early weeks of the new academic term to proactively address some of their concerns and determine whether they can be resolved at the institution they currently attend.

If, for example, they feel they haven't made friends, they might identify activities they have not yet tried or communities within the campus they have not yet explored where they can build new relationships. If among their concerns is that they are finding their courses too challenging, then they might make fresh attempts to tap the academic and other supports made available by the institution.

In some instances, going back to campus for even a second term may not be in your child's best interest, for any number of reasons. If that is the case, then you may need to take the lead in researching the options that are available, such as for a **leave of absence** or a **withdrawal**. These alternatives, and their potential impact, including on financial aid, may be outlined in a document like the student handbook, or can be described to you by someone who works in the academic dean's office or another department that provides student support.

What about a student who has engaged in all of the due diligence recommended here but remains interested in exploring a transfer?

This category also includes those who not only returned to their college for the spring term, but also remained throughout their sophomore year. One final gut-check question to ask them is if they feel they are running *from* something, or *toward* something. Of course, the response could be yes to both.

But if they are intent on exploring the possibility of setting out for someplace new, consider guiding them through a framework that may seem familiar to you both, but with the greater awareness you now have than you did at the outset of the College Conversation.

We do, of course, have a relevant exercise.

ACTIVITY #13: Back to the Future: Revisiting Those I's and C's from Your Child's First Round of College Decision-Making

As you and your child embark on this survey, we want to make two points that we hope will put the transfer application process in some context. The first is that you are not alone. The most recent figures nationally indicate that 40 percent of the students who enroll at a four-year college or university don't graduate from that institution in six years, let alone four. While many drop out, many others transfer to other colleges or universities (sometimes more than once) and go on to graduate.

The second point is one that we first heard from our colleague Marie Bigham—a transfer student herself, to Washington University in St. Louis, who went on to become an admissions officer, college counselor, and leader of the advocacy organization ACCEPT. Her advice: "Transfer is not failure."

For this activity, you will ideally have saved your child's original index cards as well as the documents containing their C's and I's. If not, you can just re-create them.

The goal here is for your child to bring a fresh eye, along with a newfound perspective and experience, to provide updated responses to the characteristics they are seeking in a college to which they might apply to transfer (their C's) and how those qualities align with their own self-assessment (their I's). We defer to you and your child to determine whether the best approach is for you each to engage in this exercise, or to leave it to them, or to do it together—whichever will spark the most meaningful conversation.

As they work their way through all these qualities and objectives, they might bear in mind questions like these:

- What do I know now that I didn't know a year or so ago? And not just about college but about myself?

- How have my responses to these prompts changed, with the benefit of time, growth, and experience?

- What values have remained constant?

- What has surprised me about myself this last year or so? And what has surprised me about the school I am attending?

- As I contemplate a change, what is it that I am really looking for and what am I trying to fix?

How should a child who is embarking on the transfer application process, in all likelihood in the early spring of their first or second year of college, set about crafting a new college list?

That search process is very much like what they went through in high school, but with the goal of creating a list that is far more concise. We suggest that, in large part, because your child will probably be filling out transfer applications as a full-time college student, leaving precious little time to do so. And their grades in those college courses will be the most important variable in their transfer application.

Your child will also have to decide whether they wish to share with roommates or friends that they are applying elsewhere as a transfer. Among the reasons why they may wish to keep the transfer process private are these: they may not get in, or they may get in but choose to stay.

As your child constructs their list, they can rely on many of the same resources provided in the section of *The College Conversation* devoted to the college search. If they feel comfortable doing so, they might also reach out to the college counselor at their high school, as well as to people they know who might be attending a college of interest or who were transfer students themselves.

Many schools will have special information sessions in their admissions office tailored to students interested in transferring, as well as more general tours. That said, it may not always be practical for your child to pay a visit. In that case, they should bear in mind that most colleges and universities designate an academic or other adviser devoted to transfer students, and your child should reach out to make direct contact. There may also be a grassroots organization of transfer students on campus who are committed to easing that path.

Those students reapplying to colleges or universities that were on their list in high school should assume that their original application materials have not been retained by the college admissions office. The good news is that the two main pillars of the transfer application process are similar to those for applying to college from high school. Once again, they may use the Common Application, depending on the school of interest, although the form itself is different than the one they used in high school. They will need two teacher recommendations, this time ideally from two faculty members who taught or mentored them in college. The transfer process's version of the counselor recommendation is a form that will be completed by an academic dean or the university **registrar**, the official custodian of university records, stating that your child is in good academic and disciplinary standing at the school and that they would be welcome to return the following term if they wished to do so.

Your child will also need a copy of their high school transcript, including any Advanced Placement or International Baccalaureate results for which they may receive credit, as well as their college transcript. The transfer application will also include spaces to list college courses taken and grades received, and the official transcript will be sent by the registrar's office. One reason these grades are so important is that they provide the best evidence of how well your child performed doing actual college-level work. The college transcript also offers an opportunity for your child to put some distance between their grades in high school and now, particularly if those high school grades were relatively weak. In all likelihood your child will be applying as a transfer before they have completed their spring semester courses. As a result, they will be required by the college to which they are applying to obtain midterm progress reports from their current professors, which can be time-consuming.

As to extracurriculars, they will include information in their transfer application about not only those activities in which they engaged in high school but also in college. Your child will have to formally request that their SAT or ACT scores be sent to the college to which they are seeking to transfer, unless that school is test optional.

At least one essay will be required as part of the transfer application. With the exception of their grades, it may be among the most important components under consideration, as it represents the best opportunity for them to communicate, directly to the admissions office, not only why they wish to leave their current school, but why they view this new institution as offering the prospect of a better fit.

As in the past, your child should keep their eye on deadlines for applications and for requests for financial aid. Unlike when they applied in high school, the responses they receive may be scattered throughout April and May. In some cases a school may require a decision about an acceptance offer before your child has heard from another institution. In such a case, your child might ask the school offering them admission as a transfer if they can extend the deadline for a response. They might also ask any other schools to which they've applied when they expect to release their admission decisions.

Once your child has received all the responses from the colleges to which they applied as a transfer, they will again have a decision of their own to make. An important piece of information as they weigh their options is the extent to which their existing college credits will be transferrable. And for those credits that do transfer, will they satisfy the institution's general education requirements, major requirements, or free electives? This information will be critically important as your child maps the curriculum for their remaining time in college. They may discover that they don't have as much flexibility to take all the courses they would like and still remain on track to graduate in four years.

As your child reviews their transfer acceptances as arrayed against their C's and I's, they may well decide to go for it and make a switch. But it's also possible that they will consider the potential new path ahead and decide, with some soul-searching, that they wish to stay the course at their current school. In that case, convey to your child that the transfer application process was hardly a waste of time, but that it instead yielded information and insight that served to provide new context for their future work at their current college.

(F.) Another Potential Transfer Conversation: From Community College to a Traditional Four-Year College or University

As we discussed at the outset of the book, there are many paths to achieving a college degree or other higher-education credential. Among the options that continue to gain popularity are those that provide a route from community college to colleges or universities that grant bachelor's degrees. Consider that 55 percent of those who earned a bachelor's degree in the 2014–15 academic year had initially attended a two-year public institution. Many of those students were enrolled at two-year schools (in California and Florida, among other states) that had formal articulation agreements with four-year schools, providing a dedicated pathway not only for admission but the transfer of credits.

We suggested that students contemplating such a path would do well early in their community college experience to determine the necessary steps involved, to ensure they are registering for the appropriate classes that would qualify them to eventually earn a bachelor's degree. Some community college students will decide they wish to reboot their education in ultimate pursuit of a bachelor's only later, perhaps even years after a pause in their studies.

If you are the parent of a child with community college credits considering a transfer application to a bachelor's-degree-granting institution, you and they will have to do some research, as the necessary information may not exist in a one-stop-shop place or format. Among the people whom you might contact are your child's college counselor from high school (even if it's been a few years since they graduated), the transfer coordinator or other faculty and administrators at the community college they attended, and friends (or the parents of friends) who successfully made such a transfer. The college to which they're interested in transferring also likely has someone in the admissions office responsible for community college transfers and perhaps an organization of community college transfer students and an orientation process for them.

We also recommend the book *Building Transfer Student Pathways for College and Career Success* (2018) by Mark Allen Poisel and Sonya Joseph, as well as the website of the National Institute for the Study of Transfer Students. While intended, at least in part, for an audience of practitioners, the NISTS website contains valuable information, along with a "contact us" link that you or your child could use to seek out additional resources. Another website is provided by the Community College Research Center, housed at Teachers College at Columbia University. It, too, is designed for an audience of teachers, administrators, and counselors but also has helpful links for students, including to additional sources.

(G.) Back to Your Child's First Year of College

Finally, let's return briefly to those students who have chosen not only to stay the course at their college but who are also thriving and quite pleased with their choice.

As they make their way through the second half of the academic year, they may find themselves already considering courses for their sophomore year. As they do so, they will likely be thinking about choosing a major, as well as internships and opportunities for study abroad.

Our advice here, as they start to plan these next steps, is that they not zoom too far ahead, although they may feel quite a bit of pressure to do so. They are still at a critical stage of their transition, establishing themselves academically, creating strong connections with faculty, and deepening friendships, including through their extracurricular pursuits. We hope that you can assist them in keeping this perspective, remaining in the present, and avoiding the temptation to race through their first year of college, given how much time and effort they, and you, invested in their getting there.

Afterword

Our conversation with you is now drawing to a close, but we know that yours continues.

We hope that the advice and activities we've offered here will be of benefit to you and your child as they move forward into their second, third, and fourth years of college, as well as beyond into work and career, and on from there, perhaps, to graduate school.

We also hope that what you've learned here will be of benefit to younger children, as you, perhaps, begin the College Conversation anew in the years ahead.

And most of all, we hope that you will take a moment to reflect on all the ground you and your child have covered together.

We leave you now not with a final exercise—there's no reason to reach for a legal pad, spreadsheet, or Google Doc—but with a few parting words of reassurance, to help carry you through these next few months and years:

You will know what to do.

Acknowledgments

We said at the outset of this book that it represented the extension of a long-running conversation not only between the two of us but with people who have been in our professional and personal lives for decades.

The first person we approached with this idea was Kris Dahl of ICM Partners, who had represented Jacques on *The Gatekeepers*. We were grateful for her enthusiasm, as well as for her guidance in helping us imagine the book as the foundation for a running dialogue, particularly between parent and child. We thank, too, Kris's ICM colleague Tamara Kawar for her logistical support, and for her warmth and good cheer. Kris shepherded our proposal to Rick Kot, the executive editor of Viking and the editor of *The Gatekeepers*, and before long we were off and running. Rick's role as a sounding board early in our process was critical, as were his efforts to tighten the initial drafts of the manuscript and to sharpen and clarify what we most wanted to share with parents. Rick also exudes an ever-present sense of calm, which served to set the tone for the writing and editing process. At Penguin Random House, we also thank Brian Tart, the president and publisher of Viking; Andrea Schulz, the editor in chief of Viking; Camille LeBlanc, Rick's assistant; Carolyn Coleburn, who was both head coach and quarterback for our publicity strategy, along with Sara Leonard; Molly Fessenden, marketing manager; Colin Webber, who designed the book's cover, and Alexis Farabaugh, who designed the book itself; Tess Espinoza, who leads the production editorial department; Randee Marullo, our production editor; and Amy Ryan, our copy editor, who got us across the goal line with her relentless precision and exquisite care.

We wish to thank Tanya Abrams, a former New York City public school teacher and former *New York Times* education journalist, whose exhaustive research efforts added invaluable context and depth to the advice we have provided here. We are also appreciative of Tanya's organizational and presentation skills, to say nothing of her ability to meet a tight deadline.

Throughout our reporting and writing, we were intentional about expanding *The College Conversation* to encompass a range of voices. At High Tech High in San Diego, we were grateful for the good counsel, born of experience, that we received from parents and their children. They included Matthew Boyd; Ariana Campos; Armando, Julianna, and Monica Mendez; Jack Montesano Acosta and Neyl Montesano; and Chloe Rodriguez. We thank Chris White, the school's college counselor, for not only introducing us to these families but sharing with us his own extensive professional guidance, honed in a school setting. And we thank Jonathan Villafuerte, the school's college readiness consultant, and Larry Rosenstock, the founder of High Tech High.

We also learned much from our extensive interviews with Harvey R. Fields Jr., Alfred Herrera, Charlie Javice, Omar Monteagudo,

Mark Allen Poisel, Jenny Rickard, and Carol Sutton Lewis. Each was gracious with their time and eager to share their expertise and perspective. And we thank Amy and Putnam Coes, who provided us with an occasional retreat that afforded us the space and bandwidth to reflect and to think.

From Jacques: I thank my colleagues and partners at Say Yes to Education, especially George Weiss, the organization's founder, for their inspiring efforts on behalf of students, families, and communities; my fellow board members at the National Association for College Admission Counseling, including the board presidents with whom I served—David Burge, Stefanie Niles, and Jayne Caflin Fonash; John Firestone, who is so much more than my lawyer, and whose friendship—and love of reading and books—have enhanced and enriched the range of my work; and my brother, AJ, and his wife, Allison, who are in the target audience for this book and who provided feedback on an early proposal.

For brainstorming and other support, I also thank Joseph Berger; Marie Bigham; Michael Dorsey; Lexa Edsall and Bob Victor; Leah Epstein; Ralph Figueroa; Raymond Hernandez; Jack Kadden; Kostya Kennedy; Stephanie Lewin; Janet Marling; Felice Nudelman; Ffiona Rees; and Elise Rodriguez.

I am grateful to have begun a conversation with Eric Furda more than a decade ago, and to have it hopscotch among various media platforms as well as across the country and around the world. I have long valued his knowledge and experience, and his passion for his work, and I have been buoyed by his energy. I have relished being his partner and coauthor.

I thank my wife, Sharon Weinstock, for her keen eye and ear, and her heart, and for always finding a way to say yes, even when my work takes me away from her and our family for extended stretches amid her intensely busy professional life. And, finally, I thank our children, Ali and Jordan, whose wisdom and insights are sprinkled liberally among these pages, always making them better, and whose good humor, encouragement, and love sustain me.

From Eric: Throughout this project I have been eternally grateful to my loving wife, Julie, who remained supportive and provided much-needed encouragement while she balanced her own career and home life, and to our son, Matt, and daughter, Liv, who shared their own excitement and pride about the writing of this book. Seeing them grow in their own lives, academically and socially, informs my ideas about and framing of life's experiences each and every day.

I am most grateful to my big brother, Scott, who, in my estimation, is one of the deepest thinkers I have ever known and who always comes through when I bounce some of the bigger ideas of life off him.

I am also grateful, and indebted, to all those I have worked with at the University of Pennsylvania and at Columbia University in the City of New York, including the great university leaders and colleagues who allowed me to grow by instilling in me a passion for higher education, in particular University of Pennsylvania president Amy Gutmann and provost Wendell Pritchett; the talented team at SiriusXM led by Scott Greenstein, president and chief content officer, who gave me the chance to have a conversation with so many parents and students on my satellite radio show, *The Process*; my partner on the show, Eileen Cunningham Feikens, dean of college counseling at the Dwight-Englewood School, for taking the leap and agreeing to cohost a radio show with me; David Charlow, my longtime friend, who has always valued college affordability and applied a commonsense approach to a landscape filled with confusing professional jargon, as well as a demonstrated ability to decode that language; and to Mark Goodheart, a close friend who served as my legal counsel on this project and many others.

And finally, to Jacques Steinberg. Thank you for believing in this idea. As an already accomplished author you knew how steep the climb would be to reach the peak of our ideas and hopes for this book. As a first-time author, I benefited from a lack of awareness of just how big an undertaking this would be. You charted the course and set the pace on our shared journey.

We want to close with a word of thanks to you, our readers, not only for permitting us to accompany you on this important and dizzying journey, but also for your openness to educating yourself about the many steps on the path to higher education, so that you might serve as a reliable and reassuring resource to your child.

Sources Consulted

A Better Chance. www.abetterchance.org/.

ACCEPT. www.acceptgroup.org/.

ACT Academy. https://academy.act.org/.

Active Minds. www.activeminds.org/.

A Degree with a Guarantee. https://adegreewithaguarantee.com/en-us/.

American Association for Access Equity and Diversity. www.aaaed.org/aaaed/default.asp.

Ban the Box. http://bantheboxcampaign.org/about.

Beck Institute for Cognitive Behavior Therapy. https://beckinstitute.org/about-beck/.

Beck, Judith S. *Cognitive Behavior Therapy: Basics and Beyond.* New York: Guilford Press, 2011.

BigFuture. https://bigfuture.collegeboard.org/.

Bloomberg. "Global Citizen Year." www.globalcitizenyear.org.

Bruni, Frank. *Where You Go Is Not Who You'll Be: An Antidote to the College Admissions Mania.* New York: Grand Central Publishing, 2015.

Catron, Mandy Len. "To Fall in Love with Anyone, Do This." *New York Times,* January 9, 2015. https://www.nytimes.com/2015/01/11/style/modern-love-to-fall-in-love-with-anyone-do-this.html.

CenterForCollegeAffordability.org. "College Affordability: What Does a Student Needs for College in 2020?" https://centerforcollegeaffordability.org/.

Chetty, Raj, David Grusky, Maximilian Hell, et al. "The Fading American Dream: Trends in Absolute Income Mobility Since 1940." Working paper 22910, National Bureau of Economic Research, 2016. www.nber.org/papers/w22910.pdf.

Clance, Pauline Rose, and Suzanne Ament Imes. "The Imposter Phenomenon in High Achieving Women: Dynamics and Therapeutic Intervention." *Group Dynamics: Theory, Research, and Practice* 15, no. 3 (1978): 241–47. https://doi.org/10.1037/h0086006.

Clery Center. "Summary of the Clery Act." https://clerycenter.org/policy-resources/the-clery-act/.

Coalition for College. www.coalitionforcollegeaccess.org/.

College Board. https://cssprofile.collegeboard.org/home.

———. "Trends in College Pricing 2019." Report 01469-962, November 2019. https://research.collegeboard.org/pdf/trends-college-pricing-2019-full-report.pdf.

College Factual. www.collegefactual.com/.

College Promise Campaign. "About the College Promise Movement." https://collegepromise.org/the-promise/.

Colleges That Change Lives. https://ctcl.org/.

College Track. https://collegetrack.org/.

CollegeTransfer.net. "State University of New York at New Paltz Transfer and Admissions Information." https://www.collegetransfer.net/StateUniversityOfNewYorkAtNewPaltz/TransferProfile/tabid/145/Default.aspx.

Common Application. "Apply to College with Common App: Your Future Starts Here." www.commonapp.org/.

Common Application. "First Year Deadlines, Fees and Requirements." www.commonapp.org/.

Common Data Set Initiative. www.commondataset.org/.

Community College Research Center. https://ccrc.tc.columbia.edu/.

Complete College America. "Momentum Year." https://completecollege.org/strategy/momentum-year/.

Coursera. "About." Coursera blog. https://blog.coursera.org/about/.

———. "How to Apply to College." www.coursera.org/learn/applying-to-college.

Crabtree, Steve. "Six College Experiences Linked to Student Confidence on Jobs." Gallup, January 22, 2019. https://news.gallup.com/poll/246170/six-college-experiences-linked-student-confidence-jobs.aspx.

Davis, Jen. "Change to Criminal History Question for 2019–2020 Application Year." Common Application, August 19, 2018. www.commonapp.org/blog/change-criminal-history-question-2019-2020-application-year.

Delahunty, Jennifer. *I'm Going to College—Not You! Surviving the College Search with Your Child.* New York: St. Martin's Press, 2010.

Noodle. www.noodle.com/.

O'Connell, Martha. "The College Search Requires More Thought Than a List Provides." *New York Times*, September 27, 2012. www.nytimes.com/roomfordebate /2012/09/26/colleges-by-the-numbers/the-college-search-requires-more-thought -than-a-list-provides.

Opportunity Insights. https://opportunityinsights.org/.

———. "Fact Sheet." https://opportunityinsights.org/wp-content/uploads/2019/11 /Opportunity-Insights-Fact-Sheet.pdf.

Ough, Tom. "Applying to Oxford or Cambridge? Our Expert Guide to Improving Your Chances." *Telegraph* (London), October 4, 2019. www.telegraph.co.uk /education-and-careers/2019/10/04/applying-oxbridge-expert-guide-improving -chances/.

PayScale. "2019 College Rankings by Salary Potential." www.payscale.com/college -salary-report.

Poisel, Mark Allen, and Sonya Joseph. *Building Transfer Student Pathways for College and Career Success*. Columbia: University of South Carolina, National Resource Center for the First-Year Experience, 2018.

Pope, Loren, and Hilary Masell Oswald. *Colleges That Change Lives: 40 Schools That Will Change the Way You Think About Colleges*. New York: Penguin, 2012.

Posse Foundation. www.possefoundation.org/.

Princeton Review. *The K&W Guide to Colleges for Students with Learning Differences: 338 Schools with Programs or Services for Students with ADHD, ASD, or Learning Disabilities*. Edited by Marybeth Kravets and Ivy F. Wax. New York: Random House, 2019.

QuestBridge. www.questbridge.org/.

Rapoza, Kenneth. "In 2019, Blue-Collar Workers Disappearing and in Hot Demand." *Forbes*, December 16, 2018. www.forbes.com/sites/kenrapoza/2018/12 /16/in-2019-blue-collar-workers-disappearing-and-in-hot-demand/.

Reality Changers. https://realitychangers.org/.

Reeves, Richard V., and Eleanor Krause. "Raj Chetty in 14 Charts: Big Findings on Opportunity and Mobility We Should All Know." Brookings Institution blog, January 11, 2018. www.brookings.edu/blog/social-mobility-memos/2018/01/11 /raj-chetty-in-14-charts-big-findings-on-opportunity-and-mobility-we-should -know/.

Renzulli, Kerri Anne. "15 Jobs That Pay More Than $75,000 That You Can Get Without a Bachelor's Degree." CNBC, January 26, 2019. www.cnbc.com/2019/01 /25/tk-jobs-that-pay-more-than-75000-that-you-can-get-without-a-bachelors -degree.html.

Richman, Talia. "Baltimore Schools' Vocational Programs Fail to Live Up to Promise, Report Says." *Baltimore Sun*, February 19, 2019. www.baltimoresun.com/news /maryland/education/k-12/bs-md-ci-cte-study-20190213-story.html.

Say Yes to Education. https://sayyestoeducation.org/.

ScholarMatch. https://scholarmatch.org/.

Scoir College Network. www.scoir.com.

Ditkowsky, Alexis. "For Families: Conversation Starters for Creating a Sane, Healthy College Admissions Process with Your Teen." Making Caring Common Project, October 10, 2018. https://mcc.gse.harvard.edu/resources-for-families/conversation -starters-for-creating-a-sane-healthy-college-admissions-process-with-your -teen.

———. "Press Release: New Report Calls on Parents and High Schools to Put Ethical Character at the Center of College Admissions." Making Caring Common Project, March 17, 2019. https://mcc.gse.harvard.edu/whats-new/press-release -new-report-calls-on-parents-and-high-schools-to-put-ethical-character-at-the -center-of-college-admissions.

EducationUSA. https://educationusa.state.gov/.

———. "Your 5 Steps to U.S. Study." February 24, 2015. https://educationusa.state .gov/your-5-steps-us-study.

Federal Student Aid. "Apply for Financial Aid." https://studentaid.gov/h/apply-for -aid/fafsa/.

———. "Loan Simulator." https://studentaid.gov/loan-simulator/.

Fiske, Edward B. *Fiske Guide to Colleges 2020*. Naperville, IL: Sourcebooks, 2019.

Florida Department of Education. "Postsecondary Articulation Agreements." August 24, 2017. www.fldoe.org/policy/articulation/articulation-agreements.stml.

Forbes. "America's Top Colleges 2019." www.forbes.com/top-colleges/.

Frank. https://withfrank.org/.

———. "Security." https://withfrank.org/security/.

Furda, Eric J. *Page 217* (blog). www.page217.org/.

———. *The Process*. SoundCloud. https://soundcloud.com/siriusxmentertainment /sets/the-process.

Georgia Department of Education. "Recommended High School Courses for College-Bound Students." www.gadoe.org/Curriculum-Instruction-and-Assessment /Special-Education-Services/Documents/Recommendations%20for%20College %20Bound%20Students.pdf.

Georgia Student Finance Commission. "HOPE Scholarship." www.gafutures.org /hope-state-aid-programs/hope-zell-miller-scholarships/hope-scholarship/.

Gillihan, Seth J. "Therapy Without a Therapist?" *Psychology Today*, September 13, 2016. www.psychologytoday.com/blog/think-act-be/201609/therapy-without -therapist.

Gladwell, Malcolm. "The Trouble with College Rankings." *New Yorker*, February 7, 2011. www.newyorker.com/magazine/2011/02/14/the-order-of-things.

Glynn, Jennifer. "Opening Doors: How Selective Colleges and Universities Are Expanding Access for High-Achieving, Low-Income Students." Jack Kent Cooke Foundation, 2017. www.jkcf.org/wp-content/uploads/2017/09/JKCF_Opening _Doors.pdf.

Golden, Daniel. *The Price of Admission: How America's Ruling Class Buys Its Way into Elite Colleges—and Who Gets Left Outside the Gates*. New York: Crown Publishers, 2006.

Goldstein, Dana, and Jack Healy. "Inside the Pricey, Totally Legal World of College Consultants." *New York Times*, March 13, 2019. www.nytimes.com/2019/03/13/us/admissions-cheating-scandal-consultants.html.

Gonser, Sarah. "With Our Shortage of Skilled Workers, Career and Technical Education Is Ready to Be Taken Seriously." *PBS NewsHour*, The Hechinger Report series, April 13, 2018. www.pbs.org/newshour/education/with-our-shortage-of-skilled-workers-career-and-technical-education-is-ready-to-be-taken-seriously.

Graf, Nikki. "Most Americans Say Colleges Should Not Consider Race or Ethnicity in Admissions." Pew Research Center, Fact Tank (blog), February 15, 2019. www.pewresearch.org/fact-tank/2019/02/25/most-americans-say-colleges-should-not-consider-race-or-ethnicity-in-admissions/.

Grothaus, Michael. "The 3 Types of People Who May Want to Consider Skipping College." *Fast Company*, July 6, 2015. www.fastcompany.com/3048024/the-3-types-of-people-who-may-want-to-consider-skipping-college.

Guzman, Gloria. "U.S. Median Household Income Up in 2018 from 2017." U.S. Census Bureau, September 26, 2019. www.census.gov/library/stories/2019/09/us-median-household-income-up-in-2018-from-2017.html.

Hack the Gates. https://hackthegates.org/.

Harlem Children's Zone. https://hcz.org/.

Hartman, Mitchell. "These College Students Will Soon Discover What Living with Debt Is Like." Marketplace, April 26, 2019. www.marketplace.org/2019/04/26/student-debt-bites/.

Helm, Lauren. "Feeling Lost in Anxious Thoughts and How to Find Your Way Again." Association for Contextual Behavioral Science, Lhelm's Blog, October 25, 2017. https://contextualscience.org/blog/feeling_lost_in_anxious_thoughts_how_to_find_your.

Hibbs, B. Janet, and Anthony Rostain. *The Stressed Years of Their Lives: Helping Your Kid Survive and Thrive During Their College Years.* New York: St. Martin's Press, 2019.

Higher Education Consultants Association. www.hecaonline.org/.

Independent Educational Consultants Association. www.iecaonline.com/.

Ivy League. https://ivyleague.com/index.aspx.

Jaschik, Scott. "Survey Finds That Most Americans Say Colleges Shouldn't Consider Race in Admissions." Inside Higher Ed, March 4, 2019. www.insidehighered.com/admissions/article/2019/03/04/survey-finds-most-americans-say-colleges-shouldnt-consider-race.

———. "Justice Department Sues and Settles with College Admissions Group." Inside Higher Ed, December 16, 2019. www.insidehighered.com/admissions/article/2019/12/16/justice-department-sues-and-settles-college-admissions-group.

Julian, Tiffany. "Work-Life Earnings by Field of Degree and Occupation for People with a Bachelor's Degree: 2011." U.S. Census Bureau, 2012. www2.census.gov/library/publications/2012/acs/acsbr11-04.pdf.

Kaufman, Ellie. "Harvard Rescinds Offers to Incoming Freshmen over [ ]mes." CNN, June 5, 2017. www.cnn.com/2017/06/05/us/harvard-n[ ].html.

Khan Academy. www.khanacademy.org/.

Kirby, Carrie. "From UnCollege to Less College." CityLab, December 2[ ].citylab.com/work/2016/12/from-uncollege-to-less-college/509216/.

Krupnick, Matt. "After Decades of Pushing Bachelor's Degrees, U.S. [ ] Tradespeople." *PBS NewsHour*, The Hechinger Report series, Aug[ ] www.pbs.org/newshour/education/decades-pushing-bachel[ ]-u-s-needs-tradespeople.

Lincoln Tech. "A Message from Scott M. Shaw, Chief Executive Office[ ] dent." www.lincolntech.edu/about/letter-from-ceo.

Mazzei, Patricia. "Racist Comments Cost Conservative Parkland Stud[ ] at Harvard." *New York Times*, June 17, 2019. www.nytimes.com/2[ ]/parkland-kyle-kashuv-harvard.html.

McGann, Matt. "Pi Day, Tau Time." MIT Admissions blog, March 13, 2[ ] mitadmissions.org/blogs/entry/pi-day-tau-time/.

Money. "Money's 2019–20 Best Colleges Ranking." https://money.com/b[ ]

Morse, Robert, Eric Brooks, and Matt Mason. "How U.S. News Calcula[ ] Best Colleges Rankings." *U.S. News & World Report*, September 8, [ ].usnews.com/education/best-colleges/articles/how-us-news-cal[ ]-rankings.

National Association for College Admission Counseling. "NACAC [ ] College Access and Readiness Programs." http://casp.nacacnet.org/.

National Center for Education Statistics. "Digest of Education Stati[ ] https://nces.ed.gov/programs/digest/d17/tables/dt17_309.30.asp.

———. "Digest of Education Statistics, 2018." https://nces.ed.gov/prog[ ]/d18/tables/dt18_330.20.asp.

National Center for Fair and Open Testing. http://fairtest.org/.

National Institute for the Study of Transfer Students. www.nists.org.

National Merit Scholarship Corporation. www.nationalmerit.org/.

National Student Clearinghouse Research Center. https://nscresearchcen[ ]

———. "Completing College." March 2, 2020. https://nscresearchcen[ ] pleting-college/.

———. "Persistence and Retention—2019." July 10, 2019. https://nscrese[ ].org/snapshotreport35-first-year-persistence-and-retention/.

Naviance. www.naviance.com/.

NCAA. www.ncaa.org/student-athletes.

New York Times. "College Admissions Scandal: Your Questions Answere[ ] 14, 2019. www.nytimes.com/2019/03/14/us/college-admissions-scanda[ ].html.

Steinberg, Jacques. *The Gatekeepers: Inside the Admissions Process of a Premier College*. New York: Penguin, 2003, rev. ed. 2012.

———. "Plan B: Skip College." *New York Times*, May 15, 2010. www.nytimes.com /2010/05/16/weekinreview/16steinberg.html.

Steinberg, Jacques, and Tanya Abrams. "College Admissions Advice." *New York Times*, The Choice (blog), June 14, 2013. https://thechoice.blogs.nytimes.com/.

Stephens, Dale. "The Future of UnCollege and My Next Steps." Medium, May 1, 2017. https://medium.com/@DaleJStephens/the-future-of-uncollege-my-next-steps -c1757dd2fcd0.

Stone, Douglas, Sheila Heen, and Bruce Patton. *Difficult Conversations: How to Discuss What Matters Most*. New York: Penguin, 2010.

Strive for College. http://striveforcollege.org/index.html.

Today's Military. "Military Schools." www.todaysmilitary.com/education-training /military-schools.

———. "ROTC Programs." www.todaysmilitary.com/education-training/rotc -programs.

Torpey, Elka. "Measuring the Value of Education." Career Outlook: U.S. Bureau of Labor Statistics, April 10, 2018. www.bls.gov/careeroutlook/2018/data-on-display /education-pays.htm.

Turrisi, Robert. "A Parent Handbook for Talking with College Students About Alcohol: A Compilation of Information from Parents, Students, and the Scientific Community." State College, PA: Prevention Research Center, The Pennsylvania State University, 2010.

UnCollege. www.uncollege.org/.

U.S. Bureau of Labor Statistics. "Fastest Growing Occupations: Occupational Outlook Handbook: U.S. Bureau of Labor Statistics." September 4, 2019. www.bls .gov/ooh/fastest-growing.htm.

U.S. Department of Veterans Affairs. "Post-9/11 GI Bill." 2013. www.benefits.va .gov/gibill/post911_gibill.asp.

U.S. News & World Report. "U.S. News Best Colleges." www.usnews.com/best-colleges.

Walsh, Bari. "Taming the Admissions Anxiety." Harvard Graduate School of Education, November 30, 2017. www.gse.harvard.edu/news/uk/17/11/taming-admi ssions-anxiety.

Weissbourd, Richard, Trisha Ross Anderson, Brennan Barnard, et al. "Turning the Tide II: How Parents and High Schools Can Cultivate Ethical Character and Reduce Distress in the College Admissions Process." 2019. Retrieved from https:// mcc.gse.harvard.edu/.

Weissbourd, Rick, L. Thacker, T. R. Anderson, et al. "Turning the Tide: Inspiring Concern for Others and the Common Good Through College Admissions." 2016. Retrieved from https://mcc.gse.harvard.edu/.

Woodworth, James L. "Undergraduate Retention and Graduation Rates." National Center for Education Statistics, May 2018. https://nces.ed.gov/programs/coe/indi cator_ctr.asp.

Yale Daily News. *The Insider's Guide to the Colleges, 2015: Students on Campus Tell You What You Really Want to Know*, 41st ed. New York: St. Martin's Griffin, 2014.

YouVisit. www.youvisit.com/.

Zoninsein, Manuela. "China's SAT, if the SAT Lasted Two Days, Covered Everything You'd Ever Studied, and Decided Your Future." *Slate*, June 4, 2008. https://slate.com/news-and-politics/2008/06/china-s-sat-if-the-sat-lasted-two-days-covered-everything-you-d-ever-studied-and-decided-your-future.html.

Index

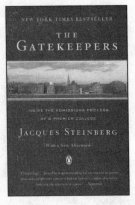

THE GATEKEEPERS

Inside the Admissions Process of a Premier College

New York Times education reporter Jacques Steinberg was given an unprecedented opportunity to observe the admissions process at prestigious Wesleyan University. *The Gatekeepers* follows a diverse group of prospective students as they compete for places in the nation's most elite colleges—required reading for every parent of a high school-age child and for every student facing the arduous task of applying to college.

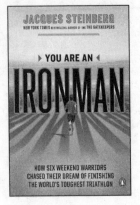

YOU ARE AN IRONMAN

How Six Weekend Warriors Chased Their Dream of Finishing the World's Toughest Triathlon

A compelling portrait of people obsessed with reaching a life-defining goal, the Ironman triathlon. Vividly capturing the grueling preparation and spectacular feats of human endurance, Steinberg plumbs the physical and emotional toll on the participants of the Ford Ironman Arizona 2009. *You Are an Ironman* is both a riveting sports narrative and a fascinating study of what makes these athletes keep going.

PENGUIN BOOKS